M000169001

Mental Arithmetic 2

Answers

Schofield & Sims

TEACHER'S NOTES

Introduction

Mental arithmetic skills are fundamental to achievement in mathematics. The purpose of Schofield & Sims **Mental Arithmetic** is to provide differentiated practice tests in key areas of the maths curriculum, to be administered regularly. In addition, there is a clear focus on how number is communicated using both number vocabulary and non-verbal mathematical signs and processes.

The series consists of seven pupil books – all of them conforming to a standard layout. This ensures that pupils are not presented with too many variables at once. **Mental Arithmetic 2** contains:

- 36 one-page tests, each comprising three parts – Parts A, B and C
- two Progress Tests, with Results Charts for recording individual pupils' Progress Test results
- Check-up Tests covering number and measurement.

Parts A, B and C

Each of the 36 tests that form the bulk of the book appears on a single page and is divided into three parts (A, B and C) – the specific content of the parts is as described on the back cover. Parts A and B use pictures, symbols and simple language wherever possible so that pupils with reading difficulties will not be disadvantaged. It is suggested that one test is taken each week and that Parts A, B and C are set on separate days. Since speed with accuracy is important, a time limit of 10 minutes per part is recommended. However, you may adjust this as appropriate.

Answering the test questions

The material in each section is graded so that, before any test question is attempted, the work will usually have been covered in class. The coverage of each section is outlined on the Contents page. The term 'mental arithmetic' implies that answers only are required. For this reason, the books are presented in a one-per-pupil format, so that answers can be written in the blanks. If the pupils are allowed spare paper for workings out, remember that their responses will be slower.

Please note: You should explain to the pupils that ▓ indicates a missing number.

Marking

A separate book of answers, like this one, is available to accompany each pupil book. When the pupils have completed a test you may read out the answers as they mark their own work. If work has been done in small groups or individually, the pupils could refer to the answer book themselves.

Progress Tests

The Progress Tests, each consisting of 20 items, appear at the end of Sections 1 and 2. These are designed as timed tests, to take exactly 10 minutes each. Each Progress Test should be administered on four different occasions, under test conditions that are as similar as possible each time. So that the test can be reused, ask pupils to write their answers on a separate sheet of paper, rather than in the pupil book. Alternatively, you may photocopy a Progress Test page that has not been completed, and have the pupils write their answers on the copy. After each attempt at a Progress Test has been marked, record each pupil's results on the Results Chart provided, or invite pupils to do so themselves.

Check-up Tests

The Check-up Tests at the back of the book focus on specific topics. Administer them at the end of the school year or when a pupil finishes the book: the results will give you an insight into any areas of weakness. When the pupil moves up to a new class, the completed book should be given to the new teacher so that he or she can plan work accordingly.

CONTENTS

A

		Answer
1	$6 + 4 + 8 =$	18
2	$15p - 8p =$	7p
3	$\frac{1}{2}$ hour = ▨ min	30min
4	$5p + 5p + 2p + 2p =$	14p
5	$\frac{1}{2}$ of 14 =	7
6	five 2ps = ▨ 5ps	2 5ps
7	$5 + 9 = 10 +$ ▨	4
8	$3 +$ ▨ $= 12$	9
9	$7cm + 8cm = 10cm +$ ▨ cm	5cm
10	$6 \times 2 = 3 \times$ ▨	4

B

		Answer
1	Add 5, 4 and 9.	18
2	Subtract 7 from 16.	9
3	Find the sum of 10p, 5p and two 2ps.	19p
4	How many 5ps are worth 20p?	4 5ps
5	Increase 17 by 8.	25
6	How much more than 9p are three 2ps and a 5p?	2p
7	$1h = 30min +$ ▨ min	30min
8	How many halves in 9 whole ones?	18
9	Three times the value of a coin is 15p. What is the value of the coin?	5p
10	How many metres is	
	a 1km	a 1000m
	b $\frac{1}{2}$ km?	b 500m

C

		Answer
1	What is the sixth letter of the alphabet?	F
2	How many days are there in three weeks?	21
3	A piece of spaghetti 18cm long is cut in half. How long is one of the pieces?	9cm
4	Six chocolate truffles are taken from a box of 20. How many are left?	14
5	If one coin is taken from the coins below, 11p is left. Write the value of the coin.	5p

		Answer
6	Which two coins must be added to the five coins above to make a total of 20p?	2p 2p
7	Find the difference in length between the longest and the shortest of the lines below.	1cm

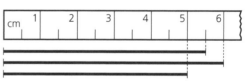

		Answer
8	Amy had 18p. She spent 9p and 5p. How much had she left?	4p
9		

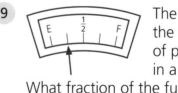 The dial shows the amount of petrol left in a tank. What fraction of the full tank has been used? $\frac{3}{4}$

		Answer
10	Josh has 12p. How much more does he need to buy four boxes at 5p each?	8p

A		Answer
1	$\frac{1}{2}$ of 20 =	10
2	10p + 6p + 3p =	19p
3	eight 2ps = one 10p + ▨ p	6p
4	14 ÷ 2 =	7
5	$\frac{1}{4}$ hour = ▨ min	15min
6	9 + 7 = 6 + ▨	10
7	9cm × 2 = 10cm + ▨ cm	8cm
8	4p + 9p – 7p =	6p
9	10 ÷ 2 = 10 – ▨	5
10	15p – ▨ p = 6p	9p

B		Answer
1	Multiply 4 by 8.	32
2	Divide 18 by 3.	6
3	Write the eighth month of the year.	August
4	Find the sum of one 10p and three 5ps.	25p
5	Write the time 'quarter past four' in digital form.	4:15
6	One-quarter of 20	5
7	Subtract 16p from 25p.	9p
8	How many half-metres together measure $4\frac{1}{2}$m?	9
9	7 × 4 = 30 – ▨	2
10	What is the total of 6p, 3p and 8p?	17p

C		Answer
1	James is 9. How old will he be in 8 years' time?	17
2	What number must be added to 8 to make 20?	12
3	How many 10ps have the same value as these coins?	2 10ps

4	Tom had 28p. He gave a quarter of his money to Erin. How much had he left?	21p
5	Which of these shapes is	
	a a square	a Z
	b a rectangle?	b Y

6	What is the sum of the even numbers between 3 and 9?	18
7	What is the total length of eight strips like this?	

cm			

32cm

8	How many 5p crayons can be bought with one 20p, one 10p and one 5p?	7
9	Which four coins together equal 18p?	

10p   5p   2p   1p

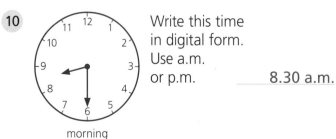

10   Write this time in digital form. Use a.m. or p.m.   8.30 a.m.

morning

Schofield & Sims

A | Answer

1. four 2ps = one 5p + ▨ p — 3p

2. $\frac{1}{2}$ hour + 10min = ▨ min — 40min

3. 8 + 7 − 10 = — 5

4. a 1l = ▨ ml — a 1000ml
   b $\frac{1}{2}$l = ▨ ml — b 500ml

5. 10p + 2p + 2p − 7p = — 7p

6. ▨ + 7 = 15 — 8

7. 5p + 7p = 10p + ▨ p — 2p

8. 2kg × 7 = 10kg + ▨ kg — 4kg

9. 16 − ▨ = 9 — 7

10. 8 ÷ 2 = 16 ÷ ▨ — 4

B | Answer

1. Multiply 4 by 7. — 28

2. Write the time 'quarter to nine' in digital form. — 8:45

3. Decrease 20p by 11p. — 9p

4. Four groups of 4. How many altogether? — 16

5. How many metres is
   a 200cm — a 2m
   b 500cm? — b 5m

6. What is one-fifth of thirty? — 6

7. Find the sum of $4\frac{1}{2}$, $7\frac{1}{2}$ and 6. — 18

8. Subtract 9 from 26. — 17

9. $1 - \frac{1}{10}$ = — $\frac{9}{10}$

10. Which three coins together make 9p? — 5p   2p   2p

C | Answer

1. Write this date using digits only. — 01 / 01 / 2016

   First of January 2016

2. Which number is 10 times greater than 6? — 60

3. Find the change from one 10p and two 5ps after spending 16p. — 4p

4. Which number is midway between 10 and 20? — 15

5. 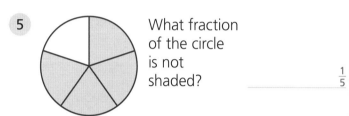 What fraction of the circle is not shaded? — $\frac{1}{5}$

6. 34 children are asked to stand in groups of five. How many children are left over? — 4

7. Find the difference between a quarter of 16p and half of 16p. — 4p

8.  Write this time in digital form. — 7:40

9. If each centimetre on the line represents 4m, what length does the whole line represent? — 24m

   cm   1   2   3   4   5   6

10. 35 is a multiple of which two of these numbers?

    3   4   5   6   7 — 5   7

6

A | Answer

1. $\frac{1}{2}$ hour – 10min = ▨ min — **20min**

2. 10p + 2p + 1p – 6p = — **7p**

3. $\frac{1}{3}$ of 18kg = — **6kg**

4. 3 × 9 = 9 + 9 + ▨ — **9**

5. 6 + 8 = 10 + ▨ — **4**

6. 18 – 9 = 12 – ▨ — **3**

7. 10 × 2 = 5 × ▨ — **4**

8. three 10ps = ▨ 5ps — **6 5ps**

9. Round 16 to the nearest 10. — **20**

10. three 2ps + 5p + ▨ p = 15p — **4p**

B | Answer

1. How much less is seven 2ps than 20p? — **6p**

2. Find the product of 6 and 6. — **36**

3. One-tenth of 50p — **5p**

4. From the total of 4, 5 and 6, subtract 7. — **8**

5. Find the value of 4 times $4\frac{1}{2}$. — **18**

6. How many centimetres is

   a 2m — a **200cm**

   b $3\frac{1}{2}$m? — b **350cm**

7. 20 plus 3 minus 8 — **15**

8. How many grams is

   a 1kg — a **1000g**

   b $\frac{1}{2}$kg? — b **500g**

9. Find the difference between (8 + 9) and 27. — **10**

10. Twenty quarters. How many whole ones is that? — **5**

C | Answer

1. How many children can be given four sweets each from this bag? — **9**

36 sweets

2. 20p and 5p. How much more to make 31p? — **6p**

3. How many minutes from ten minutes to ten to quarter past ten? — **25min**

4. Which coin is worth 10 times more than 5p? — **50p**

5. Anya saves 5p each week. How many weeks will it take her to save 45p? — **9**

6. What is the total length of the four sides of this rectangle? — **24cm**

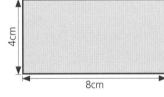

4cm

8cm

7. Which two coins are given in change after spending 25p from 50p? — **20p   5p**

8. One rabbit has a mass of $1\frac{1}{2}$ kg. What is the mass of eight rabbits? — **12kg**

9. What fraction of the rectangle is shaded? Answer using two different equivalent fractions. — **$\frac{1}{2}$ $\frac{2}{4}$**

10. Lollipops cost 9p each. Zaid has 40p. How much more does he need to buy five lolliopops? — **5p**

A | Answer

1. $5 + 6 + 7 = 10 + \blacksquare$ — 8

2. $1kg\ 700g = \blacksquare g$ — 1700g

3. $7 \times 4 = 20 + \blacksquare$ — 8

4. $44 - 9 =$ — 35

5. $3 + 9 = 8 + \blacksquare$ — 4

6. $4 \times 9 = \blacksquare$ tens + 6 units — 3 tens

7. $20p + 5p - 6p =$ — 19p

8. five 10ps = $\blacksquare$ 5ps — 10 5ps

9. $54 \div 6 =$ — 9

10. $5p + 2p + 10p - \blacksquare p = 9p$ — 8p

B | Answer

1. 500 plus 80 plus 4 — 584

2. Multiply 8 by 6. — 48

3. Share 24p equally among six children. How much each? — 4p

4. Find the sum of 20p, 30p and 45p. — 95p

5. From 78p take 50p. — 28p

6. What is the cost of six beads at 7p each? — 42p

7. Find the difference between 8×5 and 10×8. — 40

8. Add the even numbers between 23 and 27. — 50

9. Write 8 using Roman numerals. — VIII

10. How much greater is $3\frac{1}{4}$ than $2\frac{1}{2}$? — $\frac{3}{4}$

C | Answer

1. By how many centimetres is half a metre longer than 34cm? — 16cm

2. This clock is 10 minutes slow. Write the correct time in digital form. Use a.m. or p.m.

   morning — 7.30 a.m.

3. How many 5ps are equal in value to fifteen 2ps? — 6 5ps

4. Write in digits the number which is seven less than one hundred and one. — 94

5. How many strips each this length can be cut from a half-metre strip? — 10

6. If 29 August is a Saturday, what day is 1 September? — Tuesday

7. What number is the arrow pointing to? — 250

8. In a class of 32 children 17 are girls. How many boys are there? — 15

9. Which of these numbers is nearest to 80?

   | 75 | 83 | 76 | 85 | — 83

10. Divide 12p between Holly and Daniel so that Daniel has twice as much as Holly. How many has Holly? — 4p

A

		Answer
1	380 − 60 =	320
2	28 + 40 =	68
3	5p × 8 = ▦ 10ps	4 10ps
4	8 × 4 = 3 tens ▦ units	2 U
5	22 + 35 =	57
6	42 ÷ 6 = 10 − ▦	3
7	three 10ps − ▦p = 22p	8p
8	5p × ▦ = four 10ps + 5p	9
9	30 ÷ 6 =	5
10	50p − 26p =	24p

B

		Answer
1	15 plus 18 =	33
2	Find the total of 38 and 42.	80
3	What will be the cost of six pipe cleaners at 6p each?	36p
4	54cm is divided into six equal parts. How long is each part?	9cm
5	What is the difference between 14p and 34p?	20p
6	What must be added to 37p to make 50p?	13p
7	How many threes are equal to 27?	9
8	Subtract the product of 6 and 7 from 50.	8
9	A metre is divided into 10 equal parts. How long is each part?	10cm
10	Subtract 25p from £1.	75p

C

		Answer
1	Find the cost of one badge if 10 badges cost 80p.	8p
2	Write to the nearest centimetre the length of the line AB.	6cm

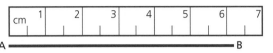

3   What is the total distance round this square?   14cm

$3\frac{1}{2}$ cm

4	Find the cost of $2\frac{1}{2}$ l when half a litre costs 8p.	40p

5   Find the total of the odd numbers.

10	13	17	18	19

49

6   Write these three decimals in order, from smallest to largest.

0.8	0.5	1.2

0.5   0.8   1.2

7	A piece of ribbon half a metre long is cut into 6cm lengths. How many centimetres remain?	2cm

8   How many 20ps would be given for the money in these two piles?   2 20ps

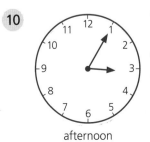

9	Find the difference between $\frac{1}{3}$ of 24 and a quarter of 20.	3

10   This clock is 15 minutes fast. Write the correct time in digital form. Use a.m. or p.m.

afternoon   2.50 p.m.

A

		Answer
1	1800ml = ▢l ▢ml	1l 800ml
2	25 + 15 =	40
3	1m 48cm = ▢cm	148cm
4	$\frac{1}{2}$ hour + 35min = ▢h ▢min	1h 5min
5	170 + 40 =	210
6	three 20ps − ▢p = 51p	9p
7	45 ÷ 5 = ▢	9
8	£1 − 46p = ▢p	54p
9	8p × 3 = two 10ps + ▢ 2ps	2 2ps
10	24 ÷ 6 = ▢ × 4	1

B

		Answer
1	Multiply 0 by 6.	0
2	Subtract 73p from £1.	27p
3	6 + 30 + 400 =	436
4	Write 845 to the nearest 100.	800
5	Write 14 using Roman numerals.	XIV
6	How many times heavier is 35kg than 5kg?	7
7	From 10 times 10 take 5 times 4.	80
8	Write the next two numbers in this sequence. 100, 125, 150, ▢, ▢	175 200
9	What sum of money is 3 times larger than 15p?	45p
10	Add one-fifth of 10 to one-tenth of 10.	3

C

		Answer
1	How much change from £1 after buying 10 buttons each costing 6p?	40p
2	How much further is it from Walsh to Ting than from Ting to Griss?	16km

41km   25km

Walsh   Ting   Griss

3	Write these fractions in order, from smallest to largest.	

$\frac{1}{4}$ $\frac{1}{2}$ $\frac{1}{10}$ $\frac{1}{7}$ $\frac{1}{10}$ $\frac{1}{7}$ $\frac{1}{4}$ $\frac{1}{2}$

		Answer
4	When two numbers are added together the answer is 45. One of the numbers is 29. What is the other number?	16
5	How many quarters of the strip are shaded?	2
6	How many complete turns will the minute hand make until the clock shows 9.15?	3
7	Ben has 9p left, which is one-quarter of his spending money. How much had he at first?	36p
8	How many times is the six in 69 greater than the six in 96?	10
9	**Stickers** large **8p** small **4p** — How much would it cost altogether for five large and five small stickers?	60p
10	If 10 plums can be bought for 80p, what will be the cost of three plums?	24p

A | Answer

1. 118cm = 1m ☐ cm — **18cm**

2. 5 × 7 = 30 + ☐ — **5**

3. 85p = ☐ 10ps + one 5p — **8 10ps**

4. $\frac{3}{4}$ + $\frac{3}{4}$ = — **$1\frac{1}{2}$**

5. $\frac{1}{2}$kg – 300g = ☐ g — **200g**

6. twenty 5ps = ☐ 20ps — **5 20ps**

7. 820 – 40 = — **780**

8. 24cm + 36cm = $\frac{1}{2}$m + ☐ cm — **10cm**

9. Round 74 to the nearest 10. — **70**

10. 1 hour – 35min = ☐ min — **25min**

B | Answer

1. Increase 52 by 18. — **70**

2. 1 metre minus 63 centimetres — **37cm**

3. 5 more than 3 sixes — **23**

4. 47 more than 28 — **75**

5. 35cm less than $\frac{1}{2}$m — **15cm**

6. Write the next two numbers in this sequence.

   12, 18, 24, 30, ☐, ☐ — **36 42**

7. One-fifth of a number is 9. Find the number. — **45**

8. Multiply 9 by 6 and add 5. — **59**

9. Find the change from 50p after spending 38p. — **12p**

10. Divide the sum of 24 and 8 by 4. — **8**

C | Answer

1. Find the difference in length between these two lines. — **$\frac{1}{2}$ cm**

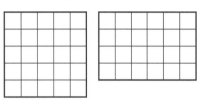

2. What is the change from three 20ps after spending 53p? — **7p**

3. Write to the nearest 10 the sum of 35 and 23. — **60**

4. How many fewer small squares are there in the rectangle than in the large square? — **1**

5. Rowan drinks $\frac{1}{2}$l of milk each day. How many litres does he drink in two weeks? — **7l**

6. Add $\frac{1}{5}$ of 35 to $\frac{1}{2}$ of 16. — **15**

7. Two biscuits cost 18p. How much do three biscuits cost? — **27p**

8.

Meera's savings		
10ps	5ps	2ps
2	2	2

Meera wishes to save 50p. How much more does she need? — **16p**

9. There are 100 pages in a book. Emily read 28 pages on Monday and 32 pages on Tuesday. How many more pages are there left to read? — **40**

10. Write these decimals in order from smallest to largest.

   | 7.5 | 4.9 | 6.6 | 7.6 |

   — **4.9 6.6 7.5 7.6**

A

		Answer
1	300 + 60 + 5 =	365
2	6 × 4 = ▦ × 6	4
3	1kg – 200g = ▦ g	800g
4	34 + 37 =	71
5	45min + 20min = ▦ h ▦ min	1h 5min
6	(7 × 4) + 3 =	31
7	£1 – 53p = ▦ p	47p
8	9p × 6 = five 10ps + ▦ p	4p
9	70cm + 60cm = 1m ▦ cm	30cm
10	42 ÷ 6 =	7

B

		Answer
1	Write three hundred and forty-nine in digits.	349
2	How much longer is 1 metre than 57 centimetres?	43cm
3	Increase $\frac{1}{2}$ kg by 250g.	750g
4	350ml less than 1l	650ml
5	What number is four times greater than 9?	36
6	£1 minus the sum of 20p, two 10ps and eight 5ps.	20p
7	Add the odd numbers between 28 and 32.	60
8	How many 5ps are equal in value to twenty-five 2ps?	10 5ps
9	Find the difference between 6 × 5 and 6 × 2.	18
10	Write in £s the cost of twenty-five 4p toffees.	£1.00

C

		Answer
1	How many 5ps are equal in value to 80p?	16 5ps
2	Which two of these numbers are multiples of 2? 41 60 57 33 84	60 84
3	How many days altogether in March and April?	61
4	Write to the nearest 10km the distance represented by the line.	70km

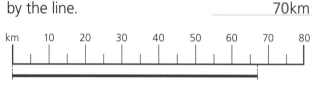

		Answer
5	Which four coins together make 10p?	5p 2p 2p 1p
6	What fraction of 30p is 5p?	$\frac{1}{6}$
7		

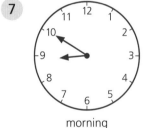

morning

7. This clock is 20 minutes slow. Write the correct time in digital form. Use a.m. or p.m. — **9.10 a.m.**

		Answer
8	Tom had 27p. He spent $\frac{1}{3}$ of his money. How much had he left?	18p
9	Find the cost of 100g if $\frac{1}{2}$ kg costs 40p.	8p
10	Write what fraction of the rectangle is shaded using two different equivalent fractions.	$\frac{1}{2}$ $\frac{3}{6}$

A | Answer

1. Write 176p in £s. — £1.76

2. 30cm × 4 = 1m + ☐ cm — 20cm

3. $\frac{1}{4}$h + 20min = ☐ min — 35min

4. £1 – 81p = ☐ p — 19p

5. three 5ps = ☐ 2ps + 1p — 7 2ps

6. 25 + 66 = — 91

7. 8p × 6 = 50p – ☐ p — 2p

8. 1km – 450m = ☐ m — 550m

9. 60 ÷ 12 = — 5

10. 300ml + 330ml = $\frac{1}{2}$l + ☐ ml — 130ml

B | Answer

1. Find the sum of 8 and 492. — 500

2. Decrease 205 by 10. — 195

3. Which number is four times greater than 19? — 76

4. Write the next two numbers in this sequence.

   250, 300, 350, ☐ , ☐ — 400 450

5. How many grams in one-tenth of a kilogram? — 100g

6. Find the total of $4\frac{1}{2}$l, $7\frac{1}{2}$l and 15l. — 27l

7. Write in digits the sum of one hundred and eighty and twenty-one. — 201

8. How much less is the product of 6 and 5 than 49? — 19

9. Find the cost of three drinks costing 25p each. — 75p

10. Divide £2.00 by 10. — 20p

C | Answer

1. Name the fifth month of the year. — May

2. How many 5ps are equal in value to two 20ps? — 8 5ps

3. Which of the following angles is a right angle? — Z

4. Find the change from 50p after buying three boxes costing 9p each. — 23p

5. How far is it from Tigby to Cater? — 37km

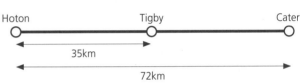

Hoton   Tigby   Cater

35km

72km

6. Write in digits the number which is ten times one hundred. — 1000

7. How much more than $\frac{1}{2}$ of this rectangle is shaded? — $\frac{1}{4}$

8. Which four coins together make 36p? — 20p 10p 5p 1p

9. Keyrings 5 for 20p | How much do 20 keyrings cost? — 80p

10. Ten mints cost 60p. How much would three mints cost? — 18p

A

		Answer
1	$(3 \times 7) + 6 =$	27
2	$200 + \blacksquare + 8 = 238$	30
3	$£1 - \blacksquare p = 72p$	28p
4	11.30 a.m. to 12.15 p.m. = $\blacksquare$ min	45min
5	$35 \div 5 = \blacksquare$	7
6	$1kg - 650g = \blacksquare$ g	350g
7	$£2 = \blacksquare$ 5ps	40 5ps
8	$17 + 18 + 5 =$	40
9	$36 \div 3 = \blacksquare \times 4$	3
10	four 10ps + eight 2ps = $\blacksquare$ p	56p

B

		Answer
1	By how much is 57p less than £1?	43p
2	Find the total cost of six packets each costing 15p.	90p
3	How many quarters are there in 3 whole ones?	12
4	How many pence have the same value as £2.04?	204p
5	Which number other than 1, 3 and 27 divides exactly into 27?	9
6	How many 10ps have the same value as £1.50?	15 10ps
7	Find the difference between 200 and 20.	180
8	Write 450 to the nearest hundred.	500
9	Add the odd numbers between 48 and 52.	100
10	a How many 6p buttons can be bought with 50p?	a 8
	b What coin is given in change?	b 2p

C

		Answer
1	How many £1 coins have the same value as 300p?	3
2	Find the difference in cost between the cheapest and the most expensive of these books.	61p

 95p £1 39p 65p

		Answer
3	If 28 September is a Friday, what is the date the following Monday?	1 October
4	Which of these shapes is	
	a rectangle	a W
	b triangle?	b V

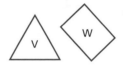 V W X Y  Z

		Answer
5	It takes George 35 minutes to get to school. At what time must he start from home to arrive at school at 8.50 a.m.?	8.15 a.m.
6	How much less than $\frac{1}{2}$kg is the total mass of six packets each having a mass of 80g?	20g
7	Find one third of the sum of 8p and 19p.	9p
8	Katie has 25p. Samir has twice as much. How much have they altogether?	75p
9	Add one-fifth of 50p to one-tenth of 50p.	15p
10	Write the missing signs $+, -, \times$ or $\div$ in place of $\bullet$ and $\blacktriangle$.	
	$3 \bullet 7 = 20 \blacktriangle 10$	 $\bullet +$ $\blacktriangle -$

Mental Arithmetic 2 Answers

A | Answer

1 (7 × 4) + 3 = _____ 31

2 ½ km + 400m = ▊ m _____ 900m

3 1/10 of 1l = ▊ ml _____ 100ml

4 10.15 a.m. to 2.15 p.m. = ▊ h _____ 4h

5 28cm + 42cm = ½ m + ▊ cm _____ 20cm

6 54 ÷ 6 = ▊ × 3 _____ 3

7 three 20ps = ▊ 5ps _____ 12 5ps

8 50p – 32p = _____ 18p

9 6p × 7 = four 10ps + ▊ p _____ 2p

10 £1.20 = ▊ 20ps _____ 6 20ps

B | Answer

1 Add 15, 0 and 26. _____ 41

2 How much longer is half a metre than 27cm? _____ 23cm

3 Add three 10ps and four 5ps. _____ 50p

4 How many 5ps are equal in value to 75p? _____ 15 5ps

5 Write 17 in Roman numerals. _____ XVII

6 How much shorter is 90cm than 1m 20cm? _____ 30cm

7 Take the total of nine 5ps from £1. _____ 55p

8 Subtract 5 from 202. _____ 197

9 Find the change from 50p after spending 28p and 18p. _____ 4p

10 Decrease four hundred and thirty by fifty. Write the answer in digits. _____ 380

C | Answer

1 Which of the triangles contains a right angle? _____ Y

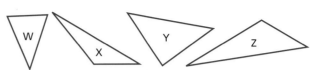

2 How much must be added to 830g to make 1kg? _____ 170g

3 How many oranges must be bought to give 11 children half an orange each? _____ 6

4 The distance round a square is 28cm. What is the total length of three sides? _____ 21cm

5 Write the sum of 500, 50 and 5 to the nearest 10. _____ 560

6 Find the change from £1 after buying 10 apples each costing 6p. _____ 40p

7 This clock is half an hour fast. Write the correct time in digits using a.m. or p.m. _____ 12.40 p.m.

afternoon

8 There are 18 biscuits in half a packet of biscuits. How many biscuits are there in a quarter of the packet? _____ 9

9 Eight children out of a class of 36 are absent. The remainder are divided into four equal groups. How many are there in each group? _____ 7

10 Find the missing signs +, –, × or ÷ in place of ● and ▲.

9 ● 3 = 30 ▲ 3 ● × ▲ –

15

Write the numbers 1 to 20 down the side of a sheet of paper.
Write alongside these numbers the **answers only** to the following questions.
Work as quickly as you can. Time allowed – **10 minutes**.

1 18 + 0 + 17 =   35

2 Subtract 28p from 50p.   22p

3 Multiply 9 by 4.   36

4 Write 12 using Roman numerals.   XII

5 400 + 50 + 9 =   459

6 What is the sum of 7 and 299?   306

7 Which of these numbers is a multiple of both 2 and 3? 14 15 18 20 23   18

8 By how many centimetres is the total of 36cm and 34cm less than 1m?   30cm

9 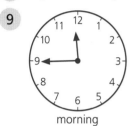 Write in digits the time this clock will show in $1\frac{1}{2}$ hours.
Use a.m. or p.m.   1.15 p.m.

morning

10 One-fifth of Noah's pocket money is 15p. How much pocket money does he receive altogether?   75p

11 How many 10ps have the same value as £4.80?   48

12 If 53 sweets are shared equally among six children, how many sweets will be left over?   5

13 How much change from £1 do you get after buying two toy cars costing 33p and 28p?   39p

14   How much less than 1l are the total contents of these two cans?   80ml

15 Find the difference in value between $\frac{1}{10}$ of £1 and $\frac{1}{5}$ of 45p.   1p

16 Ali put eight stickers on each of six pages and had seven stickers left. How many stickers had he altogether?   55

17 Out of a present of £1.20, Hina's share is $\frac{3}{4}$ and Poppy has the remainder. How much money does Poppy receive?   30p

18 Sita changed these coins for 10ps. How many did she get?   4 10ps

 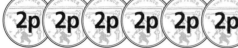 

19 By how many grams is the total of 200g, 250g and 400g more than $\frac{1}{2}$ kg?   350g

20 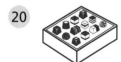 There are two layers of chocolates in this box. How many chocolates are there altogether?   24

*From: **Mental Arithmetic 2 Answers**. Copyright © Schofield & Sims Ltd, 2016. This page may be photocopied after purchase.*

PROGRESS TEST 1 | Results Chart

You will work through Progress Test 1 at **four** different times – once at the end of Section 1, then again after you have completed each of Section 2 Test 4, Test 8 and Test 11.

When you first complete the test:

a colour the first column to show the number of answers correct out of 20

b enter the date.

Each time you take the test, enter the result and the date in the marked columns.

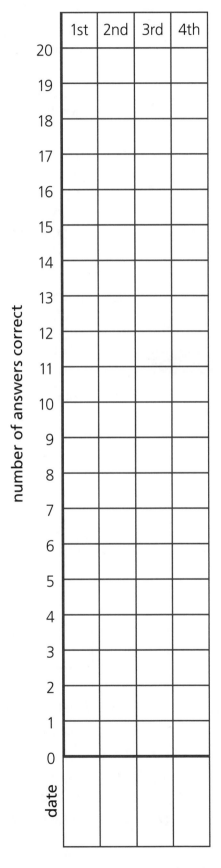

From: **Mental Arithmetic 2 Answers**. Copyright © Schofield & Sims Ltd, 2016. This page may be photocopied after purchase.

Schofield & Sims

A | Answer

1 $600 + 8 + 50 =$ _____ 658

2 Write in digits two hundred and five. _____ 205

3 $1 - \frac{7}{10} =$ _____ $\frac{3}{10}$

4 $276p = £$ ▨ _____ £2.76

5 $540 + 61 =$ _____ 601

6 Write eleven 10ps in £s. _____ £1.10

7 $8 \times 7 = 50 +$ ▨ _____ 6

8 a $1cm =$ ▨ mm _____ a 10mm

   b $10cm =$ ▨ mm _____ b 100mm

9 2 hours = ▨ minutes _____ 120min

10 $£1 - £0.75 =$ ▨ p _____ 25p

B | Answer

1 What is 580mm in centimetres? _____ 58cm

2 How many days are there in the sixth month of the year? _____ 30

3 25 groups of four. How many altogether? _____ 100

4 Write £2.49 to the nearest £. _____ £2.00

5 Multiply 50mm by 9. _____ 450mm

6 Find the difference between $\frac{1}{2}$km and 370m. _____ 130m

7 What is the total of £0.65 and £0.45? _____ £1.10

8 Share £4.00 equally among eight children. How much each? _____ 50p

9 Subtract 30 from 501. _____ 471

10 Find the sum of ten 20ps and five 10ps. _____ £2.50

C | Answer

1 What fraction of the shape is shaded? _____ $\frac{5}{8}$

2 Find the change from £1 after buying 3l at 30p per litre. _____ 10p

3 How many children can each have 10p out of £3.50? _____ 35

4 How much less than 20p is the total of these coins? _____ 1p

5 Shiv has £4 and Freya has £1. If they share their money equally, how much does each have? _____ £2.50

6 Write in millimetres the length of a line 10 times as long as the line below. _____ 800mm

8cm

7 $6 \overline{)\ \blacksquare\blacksquare}$ ← $1\ 1$ Find the missing number. _____ 66

8 | 131 | |
    | | 84 |
    | 60 | |
    | | 49 |

   Add together the numbers in the box which are multiples of 2. _____ 144

9 What is the missing number?

   ▨ $\times 9 = 6 \times 3$ _____ 2

10 How many times longer is the length of this rectangle than the width? _____ 5

$3\frac{1}{2}$cm

7mm

A		Answer
1	670 ÷ 10 =	67
2	37 + 73 =	110
3	401 − 6 =	395
4	42 ÷ 7 =	6
5	8 × 0 × 7 =	0
6	four 50ps + five 20ps = £ ▢	£3
7	£1.86 = ▢ 10ps + 6p	18 10ps
8	9p × 8 = ▢ 10ps + 2p	7 10ps
9	£1.50 = £1.28 + ▢ p	22p
10	350m + $\frac{1}{2}$km = ▢ m	850m

B		Answer
1	Add 15 to 790.	805
2	How many sevens are there in sixty-three?	9
3	From 310 subtract 30.	280
4	What is the cost of 5kg at 9p for 1kg?	45p
5	How much less than £1.50 is 70p?	80p
6	6m cost £3.00. What is the cost of 1m?	50p
7	Add 30 to 395.	425
8	25cm multiplied by 8 = ▢ m	2m
9	Increase $\frac{1}{2}$ l by 600ml.	1l 100ml
10	Take 29p from 76p.	47p

C		Answer
1	One-eighth of a number is 5. What is the number?	40
2	Half a kilogram of cheese costs €2.80. What will be the cost of $\frac{1}{4}$ kg?	€1.40
3	These are two children's scores in three tests. How many more in total did Dylan score than Eva?	3

Eva	Dylan
7, 9, 5	8, 7, 9

C		Answer
4	Divide the sum of 20 and 28 by 8.	6
5	How many tenths are equal to	
	a one-fifth	a $\frac{2}{10}$
	b three-fifths?	b $\frac{6}{10}$
6	$7{\overline{)\,8\,}}$ ▢ ▢ Find the missing number.	56
7	By how much is $\frac{1}{3}$ of £1.50 less than $\frac{1}{2}$ of £1.20?	10p
8	By how many millimetres is the distance round square A greater than the distance round square B?	40mm

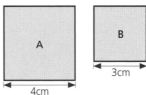

C		Answer
9	Sophie's birthday is in November. Jack's birthday is four months later. In which month is Jack's birthday?	March
10	How many metres less than 10km is the distance from Mere to Linden as shown on the map?	500m

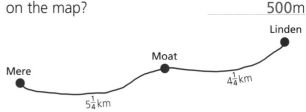

19

A | Answer

1. 3800ml = ☐ l ☐ ml — 3l 800ml
2. £3.00 − £1.60 = — £1.40
3. £7 + five 10ps + 7p = £☐ — £7.57
4. seven 50ps = £☐ — £3.50
5. (8 × 8) + 6 = — 70
6. $\frac{1}{4}$ of 1m = ☐ cm — 25cm
7. 705 − 40 = — 665
8. From 9.05 a.m. to 10.25 a.m. = ☐ min — 80min
9. 49 ÷ 7 = — 7
10. 6 × 6 = 9 × ☐ — 4

B | Answer

1. How many times larger is 900 than 9? — 100
2. 7 plus 7 plus 7 plus 7 — 28
3. Write £1.44 to the nearest 10p. — £1.40
4. What number when multiplied by itself becomes 64? — 8
5. What is the difference between $\frac{1}{4}$ of 800 and $\frac{1}{5}$ of 1000? — 0
6. Add 7 to the product of 6 and 9. — 61
7. Round 582 to the nearest 10. — 580
8. How much more is £2 than £1.13? — £0.87
9. Find the total of £0.67 and 27p. — £0.94
10. How much less than £2.70 are twenty-two 10ps? — £0.50

C | Answer

1. (0 × 3) + (3 − 0) + (0 + 3) = — 6
2. Find the change from nine 5ps after buying seven sweets costing 6p each. — 3p
3. How many times greater is $\frac{5}{6}$ of 30 than $\frac{1}{6}$ of 30? — 5
4.

BBC 1
11.30 quiz show
12.15 cartoons
12.35 news

How many minutes longer is the quiz show than the cartoons? — 25mins

5. There were 400 pencils in a box. One-eighth of them were blue and the remainder red. How many were there of each colour? — 50 blue 350 red
6.

```
   10   4
 11      8
     9
```

Subtract the sum of the odd numbers from the sum of the even numbers. — 2

7. How many jelly sweets each weighing 5g are there in a box containing $\frac{1}{2}$ kg? — 100
8. By how many millimetres is a strip measuring 25cm longer than a strip measuring 220mm? — 30mm
9. How many grams heavier than $\frac{1}{2}$ kg is the total mass of the three boxes? — 20g

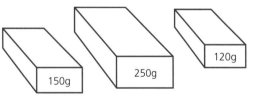

150g   250g   120g

10. Write the missing signs +, −, × or ÷ in place of ● and ▲.

64 ● 8 = 6 ▲ 2 — ● ÷   ▲ +

A

		Answer
1	689 – 80 =	609
2	$\frac{1}{10}$ of £1 = ▮ p	10p
3	9p × 10 = 50p + ▮ 10ps	4 10ps
4	869 = 800 + 9 + ▮	60
5	515 ÷ 5 = ▮	103
6	$\frac{1}{2}$ = $\frac{▮}{6}$	3
7	Round 939 to the nearest 10.	940
8	1km – 110m = ▮ m	890m
9	(7 × 9) + 8 =	71
10	43 + 38 = 9 × ▮	9

B

		Answer
1	Write the value of the 9 in £8.90.	90p
2	Write 2l 700ml to the nearest litre.	3l
3	How many times larger is 220 than 22?	10
4	Write the value of nine 50ps.	£4.50
5	What must be added to 360ml to make half a litre?	140ml
6	How much less than 100 is the answer to 12 × 8?	4
7	Subtract 1m 40cm from 3m.	1m 60cm
8	How many minutes are there from 11.30 a.m. to 12.25 p.m.?	55min
9	Add the largest of these amounts to the smallest. £2.09 £1.90 £2.10 £0.99	£3.09
10	Add together the number of days in the fourth and the fifth months of the year.	61

C

		Answer
1	56 people each went on a fairground ride costing 10p per ride. Write the total amount paid.	£5.60
2	A plastic strip $1\frac{1}{2}$ m long is cut into 10 equal pieces. How long is each strip?	15cm
3	Three notebooks cost 50p. What will be the cost of nine?	£1.50
4	If $\frac{1}{3}$ of a number is 18, what is the number?	54
5	Priya saved 10p, 50p and 5p. How much less than £1 is that?	35p
6	How much longer in millimetres is line x than line y?	5mm

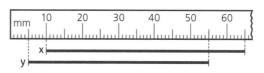

		Answer
7	The school morning runs from 8.50 a.m. until noon. If there is a 20-minute morning break, how many hours and minutes do the children work?	2h 50min
8	Through how many right angles has the minute hand turned since 12 o'clock?	2
9	What number is the arrow pointing to?	350

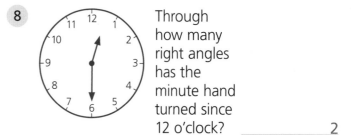

10 Four children have these amounts of money.

Amy	Megan	Tom	Sam
8p	5p	6p	9p

If they put their money together and then share it equally, how much will each child have?   7p

A

		Answer
1	4 + 40 + 400 =	444
2	840 = ▨ tens	84 T
3	18cm = ▨ mm	180mm
4	Write the missing numbers in this sequence. 750, 800, 850, 900, ▨ , ▨	950 1000
5	$\frac{3}{4}$h − 20min = ▨ min	25min
6	(9 × 0) + 3 =	3
7	$2\frac{1}{2}$kg × 7 =	$17\frac{1}{2}$kg
8	£3 = ▨ 20ps	15 20ps
9	a $\frac{1}{8}$ of 40 b $\frac{3}{8}$ of 40	a 5 b 15
10	£1.50 ÷ 6 = ▨ p	25p

B

		Answer
1	8 plus 8 plus 8 plus 8 equals	32
2	Write 5m 60cm to the nearest metre.	6m
3	Write the fifteenth of September 2014 in digits.	15 / 09 / 2014
4	Multiply 38p by 10.	£3.80
5	How many sevens in seven hundred?	100
6	$2\frac{1}{2}$ minus $1\frac{3}{4}$ =	$\frac{3}{4}$
7	How much change from 50p after buying six 8p raffle tickets?	2p
8	Add together 15, 0 and 17.	32
9	Find the difference between 719 and 735.	16
10	Which number is nine times larger than 7?	63

C

		Answer
1	Which of these angles is an obtuse angle?	X

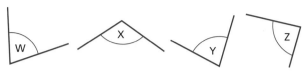

2	Find the cost of 150cm of material at 80p a metre.	£1.20
3	Jacob buys four DVDs at £9 each. How much change has he from a £50 note?	£14
4	Hassan's father is 36 years old. Hassan is one-quarter as old. How old will Hassan be in five years' time?	14
5	Samina had £1 worth of 5ps and £1 worth of 10ps. How many coins had she altogether?	30
6	Ravi is 90cm tall. Grace is one and a half times his height. How tall is Grace?	135cm
7	Harry has £1.50. Jessica has 85p less than Harry. How much has Jessica?	65p
8	What is the difference between 10 times 85 and 10 times 100?	150
9	$\frac{1}{3}$ of a number is 8. What is $\frac{1}{4}$ of the number?	6
10		

10.

a	44p
b	69p
c	58p

Which amount, a, b or c, can be paid exactly using some of the coins below?   c

A

		Answer	
1	Write the missing numbers in this sequence. 2150, 2100, 2050, ▉ , ▉	2000	1950
2	150 + 200 + ▉ = 600	250	
3	259 = ▉ tens + 9	25 T	
4	£5.00 − £2.40 =	£2.60	
5	£4.16 ÷ 4 =	£1.04	
6	(8 × 6) + 5 =	53	
7	£0.15 + £0.09 + £0.26 = ▉ p	50p	
8	$\frac{1}{2}$ kg costs 10p. Find the cost of 5kg.	£1.00	
9	(8 × 9) = 7 tens + ▉ units	2 U	
10	$\frac{3}{4}$ of 24p =	18p	

B

		Answer
1	How many sixes are equal to 42?	7
2	4p × 8 = three 10ps + ▉ p	2p
3	880g + 200g = 1kg + ▉ g	80g
4	Divide £3.00 by 10.	30p
5	What is the total of 13, 14 and 15?	42
6	How many 1p coins have the same value as £4.56?	456 1ps
7	Subtract 150g from $\frac{1}{2}$ kg.	350g
8	How many times smaller is 54 than 540?	10
9	Decrease $1\frac{1}{2}$ m by 80cm.	70cm
10	1kg costs 50p. $3\frac{1}{2}$ kg cost £ ▉ .	£1.75

C

		Answer
1	How much more is 18p + 17p than 2 × 15p?	5p
2	The clock is 20 minutes slow. Write the correct time in digital form using a.m. or p.m.	3.05 p.m.

afternoon

		Answer
3	$6\overline{)7\ 2}$ What is the missing number?	12
4	What is the distance round this rectangle? (20mm, 40mm)	120mm
5	Find the change from £3 after spending £1.40 and 80p.	£0.80
6	There are 150 children in a school. Two-thirds of the children have school meals. How many children is that?	100
7	Which bag contains the most money?	X

V	W	X	Y	Z
ten 20ps	twenty 10ps	fifty 5ps	one hundred 2ps	two hundred 1ps

		Answer
8	1kg costs 80p. What is the cost of	
	a $\frac{1}{4}$ kg	a 20p
	b $\frac{3}{4}$ kg?	b 60p
9	Write these decimals in order, from smallest to largest. 0.18 0.81 0.11 0.88	0.11 0.18 0.81 0.88
10	Fairy cakes are 10 for 30p. How much will 100 cakes cost?	£3.00

A | Answer

1 Th H T U Write in words the number shown on the abacus.

   <u>two thousand four hundred</u>

   <u>and two</u>

2 390mm = ▢ cm — 39cm

3 25 + 78 = — 103

4 2010 − 20 = — 1990

5 £1.25 + £2.80 = — £4.05

6 (7 × 8) + 6 = — 62

7 60 ÷ 12 = — 5

8 $0.12 × 9 = — $1.08

9 35 + 29 = 8 × ▢ — 8

10 1kg costs 45p. 200g cost ▢ p. — 9p

B | Answer

1 Write ten minutes to nine in the morning in digits. Use a.m. or p.m. — 8.50 a.m.

2 From (8 + 0) take (8 × 0). — 8

3 Write 204 to the nearest 10. — 200

4 Write in digits one and three-quarters. — $1\frac{3}{4}$

5 £5 equals how many 20p coins? — 25 20ps

6 What is the sum of 39, 11 and 15? — 65

7 What fraction of 25 is 5? — $\frac{1}{5}$

8 24 plus 14, minus 8 equals — 30

9 Write 19 in Roman numerals. — XIX

10 Find

   a $\frac{1}{3}$ of 18p and — a — 6p

   b $\frac{2}{3}$ of 18p. — b — 12p

C | Answer

1 One side of a street is numbered in even numbers: 2, 4, 6, 8... What number is the ninth house? — 18

2 Find the difference between 3 × 10 and 3 × 100. — 270

3 What number, other than 1, divides exactly into both 14 and 35? — 7

4 How many metres less than half a kilometre is 150m × 3? — 50m

5 How much less has Maisie than Nur? — 50p

Maisie
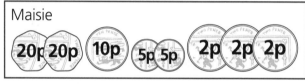

Nur
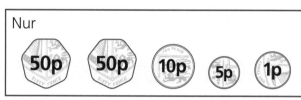

6 Three numbers total 84. One number is 28 and another 12. What is the third number? — 44

7 How many hairclips each costing 25p can be bought for £2.50? — 10

8 35cm 25cm 40cm What is the total length of the sides of the triangle in millimetres? — 1000mm

9 How much change from £1 after buying eight waffles costing 9p each? — 28p

10 Write the missing signs +, −, × or ÷ in place of ● and ▲.

   4 ● 4 = 9 ▲ 7 — ● × ▲ +

A | Answer

1. Write in digits one thousand and thirty.   1030

2. $(0 \times 7) + (7 + 0) =$ 7

3. From noon to 12.45 p.m. = ▢ min   45min

4. £1.00 − £0.35 =   £0.65

5. Write the missing numbers in this sequence.
   925, 950, 975, ▢, ▢   1000 1025

6. $(4 \times 9) + 7 =$ 43

7. $88 \div 11 =$ 8

8. Round 385 to the nearest 10.   390

9. $\frac{1}{10}$ of $\frac{1}{2}$ m = ▢ cm   5cm

10. 1l costs 60p. $\frac{1}{4}$ l costs ▢ p.   15p

B | Answer

1. Find the product of 9 and 7.   63

2. Write in millimetres the sum of 70cm and 50cm.   1200mm

3. How much is one share if £4.20 is divided into seven equal shares?   60p

4. How many times smaller is 340 than 3400?   10

5. 24p + 30p + 63p = £ ▢   £1.17

6. How many hours from 9 a.m. to 9 p.m.?   12h

7. Take 600ml from $1\frac{1}{2}$ l.   900ml

8. What number when multiplied by itself becomes 81?   9

9. Subtract 6 times 7 from 50.   8

10. Increase £2.50 by $\frac{1}{6}$ of £3.00.   £3.00

C | Answer

1. Which of these angles is an acute angle?   V

 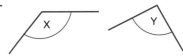

2. Write these fractions in order, from smallest to largest.

   | $\frac{7}{9}$ | $\frac{5}{9}$ | $\frac{1}{9}$ | $\frac{2}{9}$ |

   $\frac{1}{9}$ $\frac{2}{9}$ $\frac{5}{9}$ $\frac{7}{9}$

3. Rachel was born in 1990. How old will she be in the year 2030?   40

4. 300g net mass — How many grams more than 1kg is the mass of the contents of four of these tins?   200g

5. A ribbon 4m 80cm long is cut into eight equal pieces. What is the length of one piece?   60cm

6. How much shorter is line x than line y?   7mm

7. What number is the arrow pointing to?   140

8. Lucy bought these books. £1.50 £2.70
   How much change was there from £5?   80p

9. By how many is $\frac{3}{8}$ of 48 greater than $\frac{1}{8}$ of 48?   12

10. Three stickers cost 4p. How many stickers can be bought with 20p?   15

A | Answer

1. 9cm × 100 = ☐m — 9m

2. ☐ + 150 = 1000 — 850

3. 1m costs 40p. 8m cost £☐. — £3.20

4. 50p – 17p = ☐p — 33p

5. 998 + 20 = — 1018

6. 9p + 61p + 8p = £☐ — £0.78

7. How many minutes from 10.35 a.m. to 11.05 a.m.? — 30min

8. Write the missing numbers in this sequence.

   250, 500, 750, ☐, ☐ — 1000   1250

9. 72 ÷ 6 = — 12

10. a $\frac{1}{8}$ of 56 — a 7

    b $\frac{5}{8}$ of 56 — b 35

B | Answer

1. How many 10ps equal £3.40? — 34 10ps

2. Find the total of £1.35 and £0.70. — £2.05

3. $1\frac{1}{2}$ metres divided by 5 — 30cm

4. Write £4.75 to the nearest £. — £5.00

5. One-sixth of a number is 7. What is the number? — 42

6. How much change from £2 after spending £1.33? — £0.67

7. By how many is 1250 greater than 300? — 950

8. Find the total of $\frac{1}{2}$l and 550ml. — 1l   50ml

9. Add 6 to the product of 3 and 9. — 33

10. (8 ÷ 8) plus (0 × 6) plus (5 – 0) equals — 6

C | Answer

1. Through how many right angles has the minute hand turned since 11 o'clock? — 3

2. Luca has 28p and Ahmed has half as much as Luca. How much have they altogether? — 42p

3. How many months are there in two years? — 24

4. 200 ml — How many bottles like this can be filled from a larger bottle containing 2l? — 10

5. Tomasz bought three cookies costing 24p each. Find the change from £1. — 28p

6. The arrow shows the year in which Frank Jones was born. How old was he in the year 2000? — 70

7. What must be added to the sum of two 20ps and nine 5ps to make £1? — 15p

8. $8\overline{)}$ 1 2   What is the missing number? — 96

9. Jamil had 480 strawberries. He put them in trays of 50. How many strawberries were left over? — 30

10. Six sweets cost 8p. How many can be bought for 40p? — 30

A

		Answer
1	$3050 - 100 =$	2950
2	$5 \times 8 = 10 \times$ ▨	4
3	£1.25 + £0.80 =	£2.05
4	2300ml = ▨ l ▨ ml	2l 300ml
5	93cm = ▨ mm	930mm
6	$84 \div 7 =$	12
7	£2.00 − ▨ p = £1.59	41p
8	Round 497 to the nearest 10.	500
9	a $\frac{1}{5}$ of 400	a 80
	b $\frac{3}{5}$ of 400	b 240
10	$(8p \times 10) + 20p =$ £ ▨	£1.00

B

		Answer
1	How many hundreds are there in 1200?	12
2	Write 945cm to the nearest metre.	9m
3	Add 6 to the product of 7 and 7.	55
4	Find the sum of 75 and 999.	1074
5	$3460 =$ ▨ $\times 10$	346
6	What is the total of £1.45 and £2.55?	£4.00
7	How much change from £5 after spending £3.85?	£1.15
8	How much heavier is $1\frac{1}{2}$ kg than 900g?	600g
9	Three-quarters plus a half. Write the answer in digits.	$1\frac{1}{4}$
10	Add $\frac{1}{8}$ of 24 to $\frac{1}{6}$ of 24.	7

C

		Answer

1

Which of the angles in the drawing is

a an acute angle

a W

b an obtuse angle?

b Z

2 The value of $\frac{1}{5}$ of a coin is 10p. What is the value of the coin?

50p

3 1300 people attended the school fair. If 800 were adults, how many children were there?

500

4 101 tickets costing 5p each were sold. Write the amount taken in £s.

£5.05

5 For how many hours is the office open?

4h

Office hours
9.00 a.m. to 11.30 a.m.
2.00 p.m. to 3.30 p.m.

6 What remains after taking 2kg 200g from 4kg?

1kg 800g

7 How many millimetres are there in one metre?

1000mm

8 10 pieces each $8\frac{1}{2}$ cm long are cut from a metre of ribbon. What is the length of the remaining piece?

15cm

9 Two of these fractions each equal one half. What are they?

$\frac{2}{3}$	$\frac{4}{8}$	$\frac{3}{7}$	$\frac{3}{4}$	$\frac{4}{6}$	$\frac{5}{10}$

$\frac{4}{8}$ $\frac{5}{10}$

10 Four doughnuts cost 9p. How many doughnuts can be bought for 45p?

20

A

Answer

1 Th H T U Write in words the number shown on the abacus.

three thousand and

forty-two

2 2400 = ▢ hundreds   24 H

3 £5.00 – £3.99 =   £1.01

4 80min + 40min = ▢h ▢min   2h 0min

5 $2\frac{1}{2}$kg + 600g = ▢kg ▢g   3kg 100g

6 $1\frac{1}{10} + \frac{9}{10}$ =   2

7 Write < or > to make this true.

1.99 ▢ 2.01   <

8 (6 × 5) + (8 × 7) =   86

9 7m cost 56p. 1m will cost ▢p.   8p

10 (9 × 12) – 8 = ▢   100

B

Answer

1 2000 + ▢ + 6 = 2076   70

2 £0.35 + £0.26 + £0.37 = ▢p   98p

3 What number is 100 times greater than 11?   1100

4 How many millimetres are there in the sum of $7\frac{1}{2}$cm and $2\frac{1}{2}$cm?   100mm

5 Divide 1040 by 10.   104

6 Find the total of 37 and 25.   62

7 Write 4kg 400g to the nearest kilogram.   4kg

8 (3 × 8) equals (4 × ▢)   6

9 Subtract 20 plus 16 from 50.   14

10 9)̄▢▢ 7   Find the missing number.   63

C

Answer

1 Which of these is a pair of parallel lines?   d

2 Saba saves 20p each week. How long will it take her to save £4?   20wk

3 A baguette is $\frac{1}{2}$m long. How many centimetres does another baguette measure which is one and a half times as long?   75cm

4  How much change from a £5 note after buying three aeroplanes?   50p

5 Which of these numbers is a multiple of 9?

| 28 | 49 | 56 | 63 | 71 |

63

6 Four cards cost 12p. How much will 12 cards cost?   36p

7 Write the coordinates of point A (▢ , ▢).   (3, 2)

8 Write the next two numbers in the sequence.

0.06, 0.07, 0.08, 0.09, ▢, ▢   0.10 0.11
(or 0.1)

9 There were 900 sweets in the jar. These were the estimates.

Ana	Zarak	Zoe	Leo
870	926	860	933

Who made the best estimate?   Zarak

10 Flowers cost 70p for 10. What is the cost of 15 flowers?   £1.05

A		Answer
1	$3000 + 6 + 50 + 400 =$	3456
2	$200g \times 7 =$ ▨ kg ▨ g	1kg 400g
3	$(5cm \times 3) - 12\frac{1}{2}cm =$	$2\frac{1}{2}$ cm
4	£4.50 = ▨ 10ps	45 10ps
5	$1 - \frac{5}{8} =$	$\frac{3}{8}$
6	Find the number of hours from 11.30 a.m. to 3.30 p.m.	4h
7	$(7 \times 6) + 4 =$	46
8	$\frac{1}{9}$ of 27 =	3
9	six 2ps + six 5ps = ▨ p	42p
10	$72 \div 12 =$	6

B		Answer
1	How many 100s in 4000?	40
2	Write 176mm as centimetres and millimetres.	17cm 6mm
3	How much greater is (3×10) than (4×7)?	2
4	Share 75p equally among 5 children. What is one share?	15p
5	How much more is £3 than £2.23?	77p
6	Multiply the product of 4 and 5 by 8.	160
7	Write 3km 600m to the nearest kilometre.	4km
8	Continue this sequence. 36, 45, 54, ▨ , ▨	63 72
9	Find the cost of $1\frac{1}{4}$ kg if 1kg costs £0.40.	£0.50
10	How many minutes from 10.45 a.m. to 11.25 a.m.?	40min

C		Answer
1	How much further than $1\frac{1}{2}$ kilometres is it from A to C?	300m

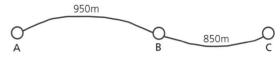

2	Eight guinea pigs each have a mass of 900g. How many grams less than $7\frac{1}{2}$ kg is this?	300g
3	What is the smallest number that can be added to 74 to make a number exactly divisible by 9?	7
4	What fraction of the whole strip is a shaded b unshaded?	a $\frac{7}{10}$ b $\frac{3}{10}$

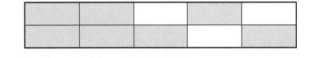

5	Three books were bought costing £1.25, £1.15 and £1.10. What coin was given in change from four £1 coins?	50p
6	What number is the arrow pointing to?	770

700 ↓ 800

7	Write these decimals in order, from smallest to largest. 0.45 0.39 0.54 0.49	0.39 0.45 0.49 0.54
8	Two gift labels and a card cost 35p. If the card costs 15p, how much did each label cost?	10p
9	475g 530g 480g 523g Which of the masses is nearest to half a kilogram?	480g
10	£3.45 £1.46 £2.54 £1.55 Which two amounts in the box total £5?	£3.45 £1.55

Write the numbers 1 to 20 down the side of a sheet of paper.
Write alongside these numbers the **answers only** to the following questions.
Work as quickly as you can. Time allowed – **10 minutes**.

1 $18 + \blacksquare = 31$ 13

2 $\frac{1}{8}$ of 56 =   7

3 $2000 + 300 + 5 =$ 2305

4   Subtract 6 from 1005.   999

5   10 rulers each measuring 30cm are placed end to end.
Find the total length of the rulers in metres.   3m

6   How many metres less than $\frac{1}{2}$km is 380m?   120m

7   How many 10ps are equal in value to £4.30?   43 10ps

8   Write £2.75 to the nearest 10p.   £2.80

9   Find the difference in millilitres between 675ml and half a litre.   175ml

10   How many days altogether in the 5th and 6th months of the year?   61

11   Which two coins must be added to those shown to make a total of £3?   50p and 10p

12   If half a kilogram of toffee costs 75p, how much will 100g cost?   15p

13   An office opens at 9.30 a.m. and closes at 4.30 p.m. How many hours is it open?   7h

14   If £4.00 is shared equally among five children, how much does each get?   80p

15 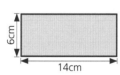 How much greater is the distance around the rectangle than the distance around the square? Write the answer in millimetres.   20mm

16   There were 7l of oil in a can. How many litres and millilitres remain when 700ml are used?   6l 300ml

17   How many 8cm lengths can be cut from a strip half a metre long?   6

18   How much change from a £5 note after spending £1.50 and £2.30?   £1.20

19
```
                    200m
    ■◄─────────────────────────────►■
Sita's home                       school
```
Sita walks to school in the morning and returns in the evening.
How many kilometres does she walk in 5 days?   2km

20   Six bags of popcorn of equal mass together have a mass of 1kg 200g.
What is the mass of four of the bags of popcorn?   800g

*From: **Mental Arithmetic 2 Answers**. Copyright © Schofield & Sims Ltd, 2016. This page may be photocopied after purchase.*

You will work through Progress Test 2 at **four** different times – once at the end of Section 2, then again after you have completed each of Section 3 Test 4, Test 8 and Test 12.

When you first complete the test:

a colour the first column to show the number of answers correct out of 20

b enter the date.

Each time you take the test, enter the result and the date in the marked columns.

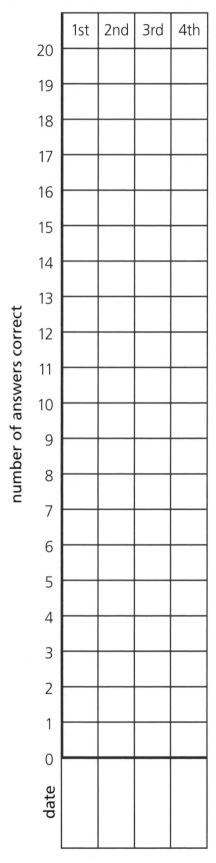

From: **Mental Arithmetic 2 Answers**. Copyright © Schofield & Sims Ltd, 2016. This page may be photocopied after purchase.

A | Answer

1. $300 + 6000 + 80 =$ — 6380

2. $6940 ÷ 10 =$ — 694

3. $9 + 9 + 9 + 9 + 9 + 9 + 9 =$ — 63

4. Write 4300g to the nearest kg. — 4kg

5. $2\frac{1}{2}$kg – 800g = ▢ kg ▢ g — 1kg 700g

6. €0.18 × 6 = — €1.08

7. $1\frac{1}{2}$m – 90cm = ▢ cm — 60cm

8. £1.00 – 58p = ▢ p — 42p

9. $\frac{3}{4}$ of 40p = — 30p

10. £1.08 ÷ 9 = ▢ p — 12p

B | Answer

1. How many hundreds in 3000? — 30

2. Find the sum of £1.15 and £2.85. — £4.00

3. IV and IX are numbers written in Roman numerals. Find their total and write it in Roman numerals. — XIII

4. Write 497 to the nearest 10. — 500

5. From £3 take £2.22. — 78p

6. Find the total cost of five breadrolls each costing 22p. — £1.10

7. 3407m = 3km ▢ m — 407m

8. What is the product of 9 and 13? — 117

9. Multiply (3 × 3) by 3. — 27

10. From 1070mm take 20cm. — 870mm

C | Answer

1. £1.35 was given in change after spending £3.65. What amount had been given to the shopkeeper? — £5.00

2. [35mm square] Find the distance round the square in centimetres. — 14cm

3. If 100g of chocolate costs 80p, how much will 250g cost? — £2.00

4. 20 drinks can be made from a bottle of squash. How many bottles will be needed for 160 drinks? — 8

5. From the sum of the even numbers in the box subtract the sum of the odd numbers.

   | 42 | 47 | 50 | 43 |

   — 2

6. Jamie spends 24 minutes altogether each day travelling to and from school. How many hours is this from Monday to Friday? — 2h

7. Write the next two numbers in this sequence.

   1.96, 1.97, 1.98, 1.99, ▢, ▢ — 2.00 2.01 (or 2)

8. This line represents 100km. What do 3cm on the line represent?

   cm — 60km

9. How much less is $\frac{1}{2}$ of £1.20 than $\frac{3}{4}$ of £1.20? — 30p

10. 1l of water has a mass of 1kg. Find the mass in kilograms of the water contained in the three jugs. — $1\frac{1}{2}$kg

A | Answer

1	$28 \times 10 =$	280
2	196mm = ▓ cm ▓ mm	19cm 6mm
3	$1 - \frac{3}{8} =$	$\frac{5}{8}$
4	£5 − £4.85 =	£0.15
5	2kg 600g + 800g = ▓ kg ▓ g	3kg 400g
6	$\frac{1}{4}$ of £4.16 =	£1.04
7	2km 90m = ▓ m	2090m
8	$(7 \times 3) + (7 + 3) =$	31
9	8p × 7 = 60p − ▓ p	4p
10	£4.90 ÷ 7 = ▓ p	70p

B | Answer

1. Find the change from £2 after spending £1.24. — 76p

2. What is the product of 8 and 50? — 400

3. 2300 equals 23 times ▓ — 100

4. What fraction of the rectangle is shaded? — $\frac{5}{6}$

5. Write 85mm to the nearest centimetre. — 9cm

6. Eight pencils cost 72p. What is the cost of one? — 9p

7. How many 2ps are equal in value to three 20ps? — 30 2ps

8. Divide 108 by 9. — 12

9. Find $\frac{2}{3}$ of 60. — 40

10. Add $1\frac{3}{4}$ and $2\frac{1}{2}$. — $4\frac{1}{4}$

C | Answer

1. Which of these shapes has two pairs of parallel lines? — Y

2. At a school concert there were six rows each containing 15 chairs. 20 of the chairs were not used. How many chairs were used? — 70

3. Find the change from a £5 note after buying 1kg of mushrooms at £2.35 per $\frac{1}{2}$ kg. — 30p

4. The masses of three bags of carrots are 250g, 300g, $\frac{1}{2}$ kg. By how many grams is the total mass more than 1kg? — 50g

5. What is the distance from Y to Z? — 39km

```
         29km
 X |←——————————→| Y                    Z
   |←——————————————————————————————————→|
                  68km
```

6. Sam was aged 10 in 1990. How old will he be in the year 2020? — 40

7. Which two of these fractions are equivalent to one-quarter?

$\frac{2}{8}$	$\frac{4}{8}$	$\frac{3}{7}$	$\frac{3}{4}$	$\frac{3}{12}$	$\frac{5}{10}$

— $\frac{2}{8}$ $\frac{3}{12}$

8. 10 marshmallows have a mass of 50g. How many marshmallows will have a mass of $\frac{1}{2}$ kg? — 100

9. The distance round the square is the same as the distance round the triangle. What is the length of one side of the square? — 6cm

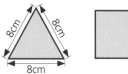

10. Alex's height is 90cm and Jade is 40cm taller. How many centimetres less than $1\frac{1}{2}$ m is Jade's height? — 20cm

A

		Answer
1	Write in digits six thousand one hundred and one.	6101
2	$9 \times 7 = 70 - \blacksquare$	7
3	£0.23 + £1.77 =	£2.00
4	73 – 28 =	45
5	£0.64 ÷ 8 = $\blacksquare$ p	8p
6	Write 378cm to the nearest metre.	4m
7	eighteen 5ps = $\blacksquare$ 10ps	9 10ps
8	$3l\ 300ml - \frac{1}{2}l = \blacksquare\ l\ \blacksquare\ ml$	2l 800ml
9	From 10.35 a.m. to 11.10 a.m. = $\blacksquare$ min	35min
10	$\frac{1}{2}$km – 397m = $\blacksquare$ m	103m

B

		Answer
1	Complete this sequence. 4075, 4050, 4025, $\blacksquare$, $\blacksquare$	4000 3975
2	From the sum of 39 and 6 subtract 20.	25
3	From £5 take £3.08.	£1.92
4	Add seven 10ps to £2.50.	£3.20
5	Multiply £1.40 by 3.	£4.20
6	Share £1.20 equally among five children. How much is one share?	24p
7	How many centimetres in three-tenths of a metre?	30cm
8	Five pencils cost £1. What is the cost of	
	a one pencil	a 20p
	b four pencils?	b 80p
9	Find the total of VIII and XI and write it in Roman numerals.	XIX
10	How many mm in $\frac{1}{10}$m?	100mm

C

		Answer
1	Which of these triangles is a right-angled triangle?	Z

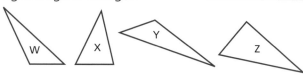

		Answer
2	Alfie was born in 1998. Jade is five years younger. In what year was Jade born?	2003
3	Holly gave six friends eight grapes each and she had five grapes left. How many had she at first?	53
4	A ——————————— B Estimate which of these measurements is nearest to the length of the line AB.	

10cm	60mm	$\frac{1}{4}$mm	20mm

60mm

		Answer
5	Which of these numbers is a multiple of both 8 and 9?	

38	49	57	72	82

72

		Answer
6	Ellie is 135cm tall and Samira is 40cm smaller. How much short of 1 metre is Samira's height?	5cm
7	257m Tom's house Sophie's house Sophie runs from her home to Tom's and back. How far did she run?	514m
8	Three of Faheem's paces measure $1\frac{1}{2}$m. What do 12 of his paces measure?	6m
9	Three girls shared their money equally. How much did each get?	80p

Abby 90p	Olivia 90p	Chloe 60p

		Answer
10	Find the missing number.	

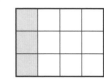 $\frac{1}{4} = \frac{3}{\blacksquare}$ 12

A

		Answer
1	45min + 25min = ☐ h ☐ min	1h 10min
2	1009 – 100 =	909
3	four 20ps = ☐ 5ps	16 5ps
4	600ml × 5 = ☐ l	3l
5	£0.15 × 6 =	£0.90
6	$\frac{1}{9}$ of 81p =	9p
7	£4 – £3.77 =	£0.23
8	650mm = ☐ cm	65cm
9	12p × 7 = £☐	£0.84
10	$4\frac{1}{2}$kg – 700g = ☐ kg ☐ g	3kg 800g

B

		Answer
1	Write 114mm to the nearest centimetre.	11cm

2 Write in digits the time shown on this clock. Use a.m. or p.m.

afternoon

Answer: 2.53 p.m.

3 Add the odd numbers in the box.

| 20 | 31 | 54 | 69 |

Answer: 100

4 How many minutes from 9.25 a.m. to 10.20 a.m.? — 55min

5 How much less than 2 whole ones are 5 quarters? — $\frac{3}{4}$

6 Find the total of 24 and 79. — 103

7 What fraction of 56p is 7p? — $\frac{1}{8}$

8 Four sweets cost 20p. How much will 20 cost? — £1.00

9 Divide £1.50 by 6. — 25p

10 What is the missing sum of money?

☐ p ÷ 3 = 15p — 45p

C

		Answer
1	In a game Josh scored 50 and 37. How many more did he need to make his score 100?	13
2	A roll of ribbon 4m long was cut into 20cm lengths. How many lengths were there?	20

3 Which of these triangles is an acute-angled triangle? — X

4 A queen was born in 1830 and died in 1901. How old was she when she died? — 71

5 Find the difference between the two largest fractions in this set.

$\{ \frac{1}{2}, \frac{3}{10}, \frac{6}{10}, \frac{9}{10}, \frac{4}{10} \}$ — $\frac{3}{10}$

6 2200 brownies were put into packets of 10. How many packets were there altogether? — 220

7 Write these decimals in ascending order.

| 0.96 | 1.91 | 9.98 | 0.99 | 1.05 |

0.96 0.99 1.05 1.91 9.98

8

| £1.50 |
| £1.55 |

Find the change from £5 after paying these two amounts. — £1.95

9 A cup holds 150ml. How many millilitres are left from 1l when six cups have been filled? — 100ml

10 Elliot's height is $1\frac{3}{4}$m. How many centimetres taller is he than Ali whose height is 110cm? — 65cm

SECTION 3 | Test 5

A   Answer

1. 5004 = ▨ hundreds and 4 units   50 H

2. seventy-eight 10ps = £▨   £7.80

3. 29 + 38 =   67

4. four 20ps – 74p =   6p

5. $14\frac{1}{2}$ cm = ▨ mm   145mm

6. Write in digits, using a.m. or p.m., ten minutes to ten in the morning.   9.50 a.m.

7. 2050ml = ▨ l ▨ ml   2l   50ml

8. £3 – 75p =   £2.25

9. How many metres is
   a $\frac{1}{10}$ km   a   100m
   b $\frac{1}{5}$ km?   b   200m

10. 49 ÷ 7 =   7

B   Answer

1. Subtract 20 from 708.   688

2. 50p minus 17p   33p

3. Increase £1.45 by £1.65.   £3.10

4. What is the cost of 25cm at £1.20 per metre?   30p

5.  This clock is 20min fast. Write the correct time in digits. Use a.m. or p.m.
   morning   6.53 a.m.

6. Find the total cost of two toy cars each costing £1.38.   £2.76

7. How much less than a whole one is the smallest of these fractions?

$\frac{1}{2}$	$\frac{1}{7}$	$\frac{1}{4}$	$\frac{1}{10}$	$\frac{1}{3}$

          $\frac{9}{10}$

8. By multiplying, find the sum of 29, 29, 29 and 29.   116

9. Find $\frac{3}{5}$ of 35.   21

10. 10 times 10 times 10   1000

C   Answer

1. Use < or > to complete this statement.
   4.87 ▨ 4.78   >

2. Five packets each contain 50p. How much more than £2 is the total value?   50p

3. Which of these triangles is an obtuse-angled triangle?   Y

4. Double the number that the arrow is pointing to.   6800
   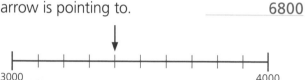
   3000   4000

5. The total mass of the three parcels is 2kg. What is the mass in grams of parcel Y?   450g

6. In 2020 Toby's father will be 45 years old. In which year was his father born?   1975

7. Each day Louise has three half-litres of milk, except on Sunday when she has twice as much. How many litres does she have each week?   12l

8. One centimetre on this line represents 500m. How many kilometres does the whole line represent? $3\frac{1}{2}$ km
   cm

9. Emma bought a car three years ago for £4869. Since then, it has lost £1010 of its value. How much is it now worth?   £3859

10. Find the difference between the sum of 9 and 9 and the product of 9 and 9.   63

A		Answer
1	2784 – 780 =	2004
2	15p × 100 = £ ▨	£15.00
3	48 + 27 =	75
4	£4 – £3.19 = ▨ p	81p
5	35p × 3 = £ ▨	£1.05
6	1kg 200g – $\frac{1}{2}$ kg = ▨ g	700g
7	7 × 9 = 50 + ▨	13
8	$\frac{7}{10}$ of 1kg = ▨ g	700g
9	9000 – 1100 =	7900
10	126 ÷ 6 =	21

B		Answer
1	Write 482p in £s.	£4.82
2	Find the cost of six notebooks costing 90p each.	£5.40
3	How much longer is 1687m than $1\frac{1}{2}$ km?	187m
4	How much greater is 1050 than 700?	350
5	Add $\frac{1}{6}$ of 54 to $\frac{1}{3}$ of 27.	18
6	3 plus 800 plus 40 plus 5000	5843
7	$\frac{3}{8}$ of 32	12
8	What is the missing number? 7 × 6 = ▨ + 12	30
9	(8 × 8) plus (8 + 8)	80
10	Find the difference between $\frac{1}{8}$ of 72 and $\frac{1}{9}$ of 72.	1

C		Answer
1	Find the difference in mass between the heaviest and the lightest of these boxes. 	800g
2	Write the missing signs +, –, × or ÷ in place of ● and ▲. 3 ● 7 = 10 ▲ 11	● × ▲ +
3	If Joel faces north and then turns clockwise through three right angles, in which direction does he face?	west
4	Lara has an album containing 24 pages with 10 photos on each page. She has 15 photos left over. How many photos has she altogether?	255
5	How many 20ps can be exchanged for the sum of three 10ps and six 5ps?	3 20ps
6	 A petrol tank holds 40l when full. The dial shows the amount of petrol left in the tank.	
	a What fraction of the full amount is this?	a $\frac{3}{4}$
	b How many litres are left?	b 30l
7	Five of Kate's paces measure 300cm. How many metres do 20 of her paces measure?	12m
8	Adam went to the museum at 3.45 p.m. He left $1\frac{1}{2}$ h later. At what time did he leave?	5.15 p.m.
9	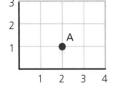 Write the coordinates of A (▨ , ▨).	(2 , 1)
10	Which two of the following, when added together, equal $1\frac{1}{2}$ kg? 350g 550g 750g 950g	550g 950g

A		Answer
1	304p = £ ▨	£3.04
2	54 ÷ ▨ = 9	6
3	(0 × 6) + (6 − 0) =	6
4	300 − 18 =	282
5	800m × 5 = ▨ km	4km
6	2017 = ▨ tens 7 units	201 T
7	140 ÷ 7 =	20
8	25p × 4 = £ ▨	£1.00
9	Write this time in digits: ten to five in the afternoon. Use a.m. or p.m.	4.50 p.m.
10	£1.28 + £0.22 = £2 − £ ▨	£0.50

B		Answer
1	Find the difference between 6000 and 600.	5400
2	How many months in one-quarter of a year?	3
3	Take 30cm from $\frac{3}{4}$ m.	45cm
4	How much less than £4 is £3.27?	73p
5	Find the total cost of eight tulips each costing 11p.	88p
6	£4.96 equals ▨ 10ps and 6p.	49 10ps
7	99 plus 99 plus 99	297
8	Add $\frac{1}{6}$ of 42 to $\frac{1}{7}$ of 42.	13
9	Find the sum of £0.29 and £2.46.	£2.75
10	How much greater is 8 × 4 than 3 × 8?	8

C		Answer
1	 The sum of the sides of this triangle is 60cm. What is the length of the side AB?	24cm
2	Find the difference between $\frac{1}{6}$ of 30 and 6 times 30.	175
3	Through how many right angles does the minute hand pass from the time shown on clock A to the time shown on clock B? 	3
4	David's birthday is in January. Charlie's birthday is three months earlier. In which month is Charlie's birthday?	October
5	Find the missing number. $\frac{3}{4} = \frac{▨}{12}$	9
6	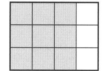 How much less than half a metre is the distance round the rectangle?	2cm
7	What is the cost of seven sweets if three sweets cost 30p?	70p
8	This line represents 300km. What do 2cm on the line represent?	120km
9	From a cask containing 5l these amounts were used. $1\frac{1}{2}$ l, $\frac{3}{4}$ l, $2\frac{1}{4}$ l. How many millilitres were left?	500ml
10	How many tins of beans can be bought for £15 if a pack of four tins costs £3?	20

A | Answer

1. 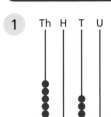 Write in words the number shown on the abacus.

   <u>five thousand and thirty</u>

2. $17 + 6 + \blacksquare = 31$ — 8

3. $860mm = \blacksquare cm$ — 86cm

4. $£3.25 - £1.75 =$ — £1.50

5. $6p \times 8 = $ four 10ps $+ \blacksquare$ 2ps — 4 2ps

6. $£0.07 \times 20 =$ — £1.40

7. $5 - 1\frac{3}{4}$ — $3\frac{1}{4}$

8. $\blacksquare p \times 8 = £4$ — 50p

9. $\frac{4}{8} + \frac{3}{8} =$ — $\frac{7}{8}$

10. $96p \div 8 =$ — 12p

B | Answer

1. How many pence are equal in value to £3.09? — 309p

2. Divide the total of 19 and 9 by 7. — 4

3. What is the value of the digit underlined in the number 5<u>3</u>06? — 300

4. Write £2.95 to the nearest 10p. — £3.00

5. What fraction of 40p is 5p? — $\frac{1}{8}$

6. How many millilitres must be added to 1l 750ml to make $2\frac{1}{2}$l? — 750ml

7. If half a kilogram costs £2.50, how much will 100g cost? — 50p

8. Subtract 18 from 65. — 47

9. What is   a $\frac{1}{4}$ of 1000 — a 250

   b $\frac{3}{4}$ of 1000? — b 750

10. In how many months of the year are there 31 days? — 7

C | Answer

1. 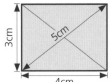 What is the difference between the total length of the two diagonals of the rectangle and the distance all round it? — 4cm

2. Chloe receives 50p pocket money each week. From this she spends 35p and saves the remainder. How much does she save in four weeks? — 60p

3. At a concert there were 200 children. One-quarter of them were girls. How many boys were there? — 150

4. How many right angles are there in a complete turn? — 4

5. Fish costs £4.80 for 1kg. How much will $1\frac{1}{2}$kg cost? — £7.20

6.
Received	Spent
£1.50	£0.30
	£0.65

   This is how Daniel keeps an account of his money. How much has he left? — £0.55

7. By how many metres is $1\frac{3}{4}$km shorter than 2000m? — 250m

8. The total length of the three sides of this triangle is 14cm. What is the length in millimetres of the side YZ? — 56mm

9. Find the difference in cost between four toy sheep at 30p each and two toy elephants at 55p each. — 10p

10. Find the total of VI and XIV and write it in Roman numerals. — XX

39

Schofield & Sims

A | Answer

1. Write in digits the number nine thousand and thirteen. ___9013___

2. 21p × 100 = £ ___£21.00___

3. 4000 = 40 × ___100___

4. (7 × 8) + 5 = ___61___

5. $1\frac{1}{2}$ l – 550ml = ___ ml ___950ml___

6. four 2ps + 27p = ___ 5ps ___7 5ps___

7. 50p – 17p = ___ p ___33p___

8. 750 ÷ 5 = ___150___

9. 350 ÷ 7 = ___50___

10. $\frac{3}{10} + \frac{4}{10}$ = ___$\frac{7}{10}$___

B | Answer

1. Take 200 from 4080. ___3880___

2. Write 5450ml to the nearest litre. ___5l___

3. How many whole ones are equal to 28 quarters? ___7___

4. 470g × 10 = ___ kg ___ g ___4kg 700g___

5. Find the product of 6 and 23. ___138___

6. Decrease 41 by 13. ___28___

7. How many minutes from 11.35 a.m. to 12.25 p.m.? ___50min___

8. How much less than £4 is £2.72? ___£1.28___

9. Find the difference between 7 × 8 and 6 × 9. ___2___

10. Arrange the digits 6, 9, 4 and 8 to make the largest possible number. ___9864___

C | Answer

1. By how much is the sum of £1.15 and 36p less than £2? ___49p___

2. Six pieces of wire each measure 9cm. Find the total length of the pieces in millimetres. ___540mm___

3. Add 1500 to the number shown by the arrow. ___9200___

7000   8000

4. Six apples are cut into quarters. How many children can each have three of the pieces? ___8___

5.
| £2.35 |
| £0.07 |
| £1.70 |

The receipt shows how much Sita spent at the supermarket. Find the total amount. ___£4.12___

6. A banana costs 8p.

   a How many can be bought for 60p? a ___7___

   b What change will there be? b ___4p___

7. Ruby is at school from 9.00 a.m. until 4.00 p.m. What time remains after taking $2\frac{1}{4}$ h for break and dinner time? ___$4\frac{3}{4}$ h___

8. One of the measurements below is the distance all round the square. Estimate which is the correct measurement.

   | $\frac{1}{2}$ m | $\frac{1}{4}$ m | 120cm | 80mm | 20cm |

   ___80mm___

9. Eight children each collected 80p and two children collected 70p each. How much was this altogether? ___£7.80___

10. Isha had £2.40. She spent $\frac{3}{8}$ of it. How much money had she left? ___£1.50___

A | Answer

1. 540 + 70 = __610__

2. (3 × 1000) + (6 × 100) + (4 × 10) = __3640__

3. nine 10ps + eight 5ps = £ ▨ __£1.30__

4. $\frac{1}{2}$l + 650ml = 1l + ▨ ml __150ml__

5. £5 – £ ▨ = £3.10 __£1.90__

6. £2.89 + £0.17 = __£3.06__

7. £1.17 ÷ 9 = . __£0.13__

8. 40 × 7 = __280__

9. $\frac{2}{3}$ of 45p = __30p__

10. $6\overline{)1\ 3▨▨}$ Find the missing number. __78__

B | Answer

1. 7 plus 7 plus 7 plus 7 plus 7 __35__

2. Find the difference between 8 times 9 and 8 times 4. __40__

3. Find the cost of eight pens costing 22p each. __£1.76__

4. Write 249cm to the nearest metre. __2m__

5. How many whole ones equal 40 tenths? __4__

6. Find the total of 65p and £3.80. __£4.45__

7. What must be added to £1.94 to make £3? __£1.06__

8. Find $\frac{3}{8}$ of 48. __18__

9. (45 ÷ 5) minus (18 ÷ 3) __3__

10. How many $\frac{1}{4}$l are there in $3\frac{1}{2}$l? __14__

C | Answer

1. Write these decimals in ascending order.

   | 3.79 | 3.31 | 2.87 | 2.09 | 3.33 |

   __2.09   2.87   3.31   3.33   3.79__

2. From a carton containing 50kg of sugar, 24 half-kilogram packets were taken. How many kilograms of sugar remained? __38kg__

3. Which of these numbers are multiples of both 4 and 9?

   | 18 | 27 | 36 | 45 | 54 |

   __36__

4. What will four balloons cost if 10 balloons cost £3.00? __£1.20__

5. What fraction of a kilometre is walked by Tom when he walks to Sam's house and back again? __$\frac{1}{4}$ km__

   Tom's house   Sam's house
   ◄——————— 125m ———————►

6. Muffins cost 7p each.

   a How many can be bought for 30p? __a   4__

   b How much change will there be? __b   2p__

7. A prize was shared among Vicky, Megan and Sanjay. Vicky had $\frac{5}{10}$ of the money and Megan had $\frac{3}{10}$. What fraction of the money did Sanjay receive? __$\frac{2}{10}$__

8. To $\frac{2}{3}$ of 15p add $\frac{4}{5}$ of 50p. __50p__

9. The contents of the three cans are put into a bowl. How many millilitres less than $2\frac{1}{2}$l is this? __400ml__

   1250ml   450ml   400ml

10. Find the total of IV, VI and IX and write it in Roman numerals. __XIX__

A | Answer

1. 869ml = $\frac{1}{2}$l + ▊ml — 369ml
2. $\frac{7}{10}$ of 1m = ▊cm — 70cm
3. 48 + 74 = — 122
4. $3.50 − $1.75 = — $1.75
5. (8 × 5) + (8 × 3) = — 64
6. $\frac{7}{8} − \frac{4}{8}$ = — $\frac{3}{8}$
7. $\frac{1}{2}$m = ▊mm — 500mm
8. 54 ÷ 9 = 1 + ▊ — 5
9. (0 × 10) + (10 × 10) + (10 − 0) = — 110
10. ▊ ÷ 6 = 21 — 126

B | Answer

1. How many fifths of the strip are shaded? — $\frac{3}{5}$

2. How many 20ps are equal in value to £10? — 50 20ps
3. Find the number of days in seven weeks. — 49
4. How many whole ones are equal to 15 fifths? — 3
5. How much more is £2.59 than £1.60? — £0.99
6. Apples cost 12p each. How much will seven cost? — 84p
7. Take 13p from 50p. — 37p
8. Five oranges cost 40p. What will 15 of the oranges cost? — £1.20
9. Find $\frac{3}{4}$ of 32. — 24
10. Write in digits, 11 minutes to 7 in the morning. Use a.m. or p.m. — 6.49 a.m.

C | Answer

1.

Scores	
Jay	Emily
19	20
11	13
10	17

How many more did Emily score than Jay? — 10

2. Double the number the arrow is pointing to and write the answer as a decimal. — 1.4

3. A train due to arrive at 11.35 a.m. was 40 minutes late. At what time did it arrive? — 12.15 p.m.

4.  three tins for 45p | How much would nine of these tins cost? — £1.35

5. In a school of 120 children, one-tenth was absent. How many children were present? — 108

6. Write the coordinates of A (▊ , ▊). — (3, 0)

7. Find the total of II, IX and V and write it in Roman numerals. — XVI

8. Guess the number | Winner 450 | In the competition, Ben's guess was 395 and Amy's guess was 510.

   a Who was the nearest and — a Ben

   b by how many? — b 5

9. How many pence less are there in $\frac{3}{8}$ of 40p than in $\frac{5}{8}$ of 40p? — 10p

10.

| 38p | 13p | 27p | 34p |

Which of the amounts above could not be paid for exactly using some or all of these coins? — 34p

A | Answer

1. $\frac{1}{3}$ of £3.09 =   £1.03

2. (8 × 1000) + (6 × 10) + (9 × 1) =   8069

3. £1.25 × 4 =   £5.00

4. How many 12s are there in
   a 120 and   a 10
   b 1200?   b 100

5. 1l ÷ 4 = ▉ ml   250ml

6. 6 × 6 = ▉ × 9   4

7. £1.59 + £0.48 =   £2.07

8. Complete this sequence.
   3000, 3250, 3500, 3750, ▉, ▉
   4000   4250

9. Arrange the digits 1, 2, 7, 0 to make the largest possible even number.   7210

10. ▉ ÷ 7 = 21   147

B | Answer

1. Round 4728 to the nearest 100.   4700

2. (6 × 0) + (0 + 6) + (6 × 1) =   12

3. What fraction of 60 is 10? $\frac{1}{6}$

4. If $\frac{3}{4}$ of a sum of money is 24p what is $\frac{1}{4}$ of the money?   8p

5. The sum of two numbers is 159. One of the numbers is 60. What is the other number?   99

6. Multiply $2\frac{1}{2}$ by 6.   15

7. Find the cost of $\frac{1}{2}$ kg when 2kg cost 60p.   15p

8. Change seventy-eight 2ps to £s.   £1.56

9. Bagels cost 8p. What is the cost of
   a 10   a   80p
   b 100?   b £8.00

10. Write in digits, ten to one in the afternoon, using the 12-hour clock.   12.50 p.m.

C | Answer

1. £1.75 £1.35 Find the change from a £5 note after paying these two amounts.   £1.90

2. 100 paper clips cost £1. How much will 70 paper clips cost at the same rate?   70p

3. How many more is 1010 minus 100 than 1100 minus 200?   10

4. Put these fractions in ascending order.
   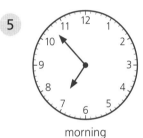
   $\frac{3}{10}$ $\frac{1}{2}$ $\frac{6}{10}$ $\frac{9}{10}$

5. Write this time in digits. Use a.m. or p.m.   6.53 a.m.
   morning

6. How many days are there in the first two months of a leap year?   60

7. Subtract the product of seven and seven from the product of eight and eight.   15

8. Halve the number the arrow is pointing to and write the answer as a decimal.   0.4

9. Find the cost of $1\frac{3}{4}$ m if 1m costs £2.   £3.50

10. How many 250g packets of gingerbread men can be filled from a box containing $4\frac{1}{2}$ kg?   18

A Write in words the number shown on each abacus.

| Th | H | T | U | | Th | H | T | U |

three thousand
and forty-three

two thousand
and fifty

B

		a		b
Take 1 from	900	899	2000	1999
Add 1 to	499	500	3999	4000
Take 10 from	6000	5990	5005	4995
Add 10 to	894	904	7095	7105
Take 100 from	1001	901	4060	3960
Add 100 to	7049	7149	6990	7090

C Write in digits

two thousand nine hundred	2900	one thousand and fifty	1050	four thousand and eight	4008

D Write the value of the digit underlined in each number.

80$\underline{1}$0	10	328$\underline{4}$	4
2$\underline{9}$66	900	8$\underline{3}$04	300
$\underline{4}$075	4000	109$\underline{0}$	90
5$\underline{1}$24	100	$\underline{5}$007	5000

E

862 =	tens 2 units	86
2307 =	tens 7 units	230
470 =	hundreds 7 tens	4
6850 =	hundreds 5 tens	68
4605 =	hundreds 5 units	46

F

1000 + 500 + 70 + 5 =	1575
3000 + 60 + 4 =	3064
4000 + 80 =	4080
9 + 6000 =	6009

G

How many times larger is		How many times smaller is	
150 than 15	10	12 than 120	10
200 than 2	100	70 than 700	10
600 than 60	10	59 than 590	10
3000 than 30?	100	42 than 4200?	100

H Addition

8 + 5 =	13	19 + 4 =	23
7 + 6 =	13	5 + 17 =	22
2 + 9 =	11	16 + 6 =	22
8 + 8 =	16	9 + 18 =	27
6 + 6 =	12	19 + 7 =	26
3 + 9 =	12	5 + 18 =	23
8 + 7 =	15	29 + 6 =	35
9 + 9 =	18	8 + 24 =	32
8 + 4 =	12	38 + 3 =	41
9 + 5 =	14	7 + 37 =	44
7 + 7 =	14	49 + 2 =	51
6 + 9 =	15	7 + 44 =	51
9 + 8 =	17	58 + 8 =	66
7 + 4 =	11	5 + 59 =	64
3 + 8 =	11	65 + 6 =	71
7 + 5 =	12	6 + 68 =	74
8 + 6 =	14	79 + 9 =	88
4 + 9 =	13	8 + 77 =	85
6 + 5 =	11	83 + 9 =	92
9 + 7 =	16	7 + 86 =	93

I Subtraction

16 − 9 =	7	22 − 4 =	18
11 − 7 =	4	24 − 7 =	17
14 − 8 =	6	21 − 6 =	15
13 − 7 =	6	26 − 9 =	17
17 − 9 =	8	24 − 8 =	16
11 − 8 =	3	35 − 9 =	26
12 − 9 =	3	31 − 5 =	26
13 − 6 =	7	37 − 8 =	29
15 − 8 =	7	43 − 5 =	38
13 − 9 =	4	44 − 9 =	35
12 − 6 =	6	52 − 3 =	49
15 − 9 =	6	53 − 7 =	46
14 − 7 =	7	62 − 9 =	53
13 − 8 =	5	63 − 4 =	59
12 − 7 =	5	71 − 8 =	63
14 − 5 =	9	72 − 6 =	66
12 − 4 =	8	81 − 7 =	74
11 − 6 =	5	85 − 8 =	77
12 − 8 =	4	91 − 4 =	87
18 − 9 =	9	98 − 9 =	89

Tables 2, 3, 4, 5, 6, 7, 8, 9

A   Multiplication

12 × 3 =	36	(3 × 4) + 3 =	15	14 ÷ 2 =	7	36 ÷ 6 =	6
4 × 8 =	32	(0 × 8) + 7 =	7	24 ÷ 4 =	6	49 ÷ 7 =	7
0 × 3 =	0	(8 × 4) + 3 =	35	40 ÷ 5 =	8	66 ÷ 6 =	11
9 × 6 =	54	(5 × 7) + 6 =	41	36 ÷ 3 =	12	81 ÷ 9 =	9
11 × 5 =	55	(1 × 6) + 5 =	11	60 ÷ 5 =	12	56 ÷ 8 =	7
7 × 6 =	42	(6 × 4) + 3 =	27	18 ÷ 3 =	6	77 ÷ 7 =	11
0 × 5 =	0	(11 × 8) + 5 =	93	0 ÷ 2 =	0	42 ÷ 7 =	6
7 × 8 =	56	(5 × 6) + 4 =	34	4 ÷ 4 =	1	32 ÷ 8 =	4
3 × 7 =	21	(8 × 8) + 7 =	71	44 ÷ 4 =	11	72 ÷ 6 =	12
9 × 5 =	45	(2 × 6) + 4 =	16	27 ÷ 3 =	9	90 ÷ 9 =	10
6 × 12 =	72	(8 × 5) + 2 =	42	8 ÷ 2 =	4	0 ÷ 8 =	0
7 × 9 =	63	(7 × 7) + 5 =	54	99 ÷ 9 =	11	108 ÷ 9 =	12
5 × 5 =	25	(1 × 8) + 4 =	12	35 ÷ 5 =	7	63 ÷ 7 =	9
12 × 7 =	84	(2 × 9) + 6 =	24	0 ÷ 3 =	0	56 ÷ 7 =	8
6 × 6 =	36	(7 × 4) + 3 =	31	36 ÷ 4 =	9	72 ÷ 9 =	8
9 × 4 =	36	(12 × 7) + 6 =	90	24 ÷ 2 =	12	35 ÷ 7 =	5
12 × 9 =	108	(8 × 9) + 7 =	79	28 ÷ 4 =	7	54 ÷ 6 =	9
6 × 8 =	48	(0 × 6) + 4 =	4	55 ÷ 5 =	11	84 ÷ 7 =	12
11 × 4 =	44	(4 × 4) + 3 =	19	16 ÷ 4 =	4	96 ÷ 8 =	12
8 × 3 =	24	(9 × 11) + 8 =	107	33 ÷ 3 =	11	36 ÷ 9 =	4

B   Division

C   What fraction of each of these shapes is   **a** shaded   **b** unshaded?

a $\frac{1}{2}$ b $\frac{1}{2}$

a $\frac{1}{4}$ b $\frac{3}{4}$

a $\frac{1}{8}$ b $\frac{7}{8}$

a $\frac{1}{3}$ b $\frac{2}{3}$

a $\frac{1}{6}$ b $\frac{5}{6}$

   a $\frac{2}{5}$ b $\frac{3}{5}$

   a $\frac{3}{10}$ b $\frac{7}{10}$

D   Write in digits.

one and a half $1\frac{1}{2}$

two and three-quarters $2\frac{3}{4}$

three and three-fifths $3\frac{3}{5}$

four and two-thirds $4\frac{2}{3}$

E

				Write < or >
$1 = \frac{\square}{2}$ 2	$\frac{1}{3} + \frac{1}{3} =$ $\frac{2}{3}$	$\frac{4}{4} - \frac{3}{4} =$ $\frac{1}{4}$	$\frac{7}{8} - \frac{4}{8} =$ $\frac{3}{8}$	$\frac{5}{8}$ $\frac{3}{8}$ >
$1 = \frac{\square}{4}$ 4	$\frac{3}{5} + \frac{1}{5} =$ $\frac{4}{5}$	$\frac{8}{8} - \frac{5}{8} =$ $\frac{3}{8}$	$\frac{5}{6} - \frac{4}{6} =$ $\frac{1}{6}$	$\frac{1}{6}$ $\frac{5}{6}$ <
$1 = \frac{\square}{8}$ 8	$\frac{1}{10} + \frac{2}{10} =$ $\frac{3}{10}$	$\frac{3}{3} - \frac{2}{3} =$ $\frac{1}{3}$	$\frac{9}{10} - \frac{8}{10} =$ $\frac{1}{10}$	$\frac{5}{6}$ $\frac{5}{8}$ >
$1 = \frac{\square}{5}$ 5	$\frac{3}{10} + \frac{4}{10} =$ $\frac{7}{10}$	$\frac{10}{10} - \frac{7}{10} =$ $\frac{3}{10}$	$\frac{11}{12} - \frac{7}{12} =$ $\frac{4}{12}$	$\frac{1}{10}$ $\frac{1}{2}$ <

F   Find the value of

$\frac{1}{2}$ of 18p 9p	$\frac{1}{4}$ of 20l 5l	$\frac{1}{5}$ of 40m 8m	$\frac{1}{6}$ of 30p 5p
$\frac{1}{4}$ of 24kg 6kg	$\frac{3}{4}$ of 20l 15l	$\frac{4}{5}$ of 40m 32m	$\frac{5}{6}$ of 30p 25p
$\frac{1}{10}$ of 60cm 6cm	$\frac{1}{8}$ of 32cm 4cm	$\frac{1}{10}$ of £1 10p	$\frac{1}{3}$ of 90kg 30kg
$\frac{1}{3}$ of 27p 9p	$\frac{7}{8}$ of 32cm 28cm	$\frac{9}{10}$ of £1 90p	$\frac{2}{3}$ of 90kg 60kg

45

A

£1 = ▦ 50ps	2	50p = ▦ 10ps	5	£1.48 = £1 + ▦ p	48p
£1 = ▦ 20ps	5	50p = ▦ 5ps	10	£2.09 = £2 + ▦ p	9p
£1 = ▦ 10ps	10	50p = ▦ 2ps	25	£0.63 = £0 + ▦ p	63p
£1 = ▦ 5ps	20			£2.80 = £2 + ▦ p	80p
£1 = ▦ 2ps	50	20p = ▦ 10ps	2	157p = £ ▦	£1.57
£1 = ▦ 1ps	100	20p = ▦ 5ps	4	260p = £ ▦	£2.60
		20p = ▦ 2ps	10	309p = £ ▦	£3.09

B Find the change.

Amount	Money spent	Change
10p	4p	6p
10p	5p	5p
10p	7p	3p
15p	11p	4p
15p	13p	2p
20p	5p	15p
20p	8p	12p
20p	13p	7p

Amount	Money spent	Change
50p	17p	33p
50p	38p	12p
50p	24p	26p
50p	11p	39p
50p	27p	23p
50p	19p	31p
80p	76p	4p
90p	81p	9p

Amount	Money spent	Change
£1	24p	76p
£1	68p	32p
£1	85p	15p
£1	43p	57p
£1	91p	9p
£5	£4.62	38p
£5	£2.30	£2.70
£5	£3.09	£1.91

C By counting, find the total value of the coins in each box.

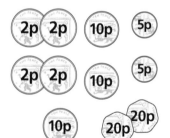 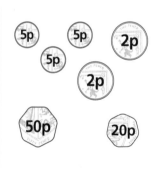 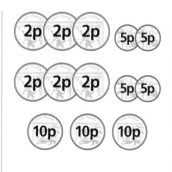

88p   89p   62p   £2.10

D

Divide 54p by 9.	6p
Reduce 67p by 19p.	48p
Find the sum of 23p and 17p.	40p
What is the total of 68p and 9p?	77p
Multiply 14p by 5.	70p

Find the difference between £0.57 and 75p.	18p
Add 24p to 66p.	90p
How much greater is £1 than 38p?	62p
18p plus 12p minus 10p.	20p
Subtract 41p from 90p.	49p

E

Write to the nearest 10p.

34p   30p   £0.86   90p   £1.95 £2.00   £3.07 £3.10

Write to the nearest £1.

£1.80 £2.00   £3.30 £3.00   £2.25 £2.00   £4.50 £5.00

CHECK-UP TEST | Measurement

A

20mm =	2cm	135cm =	1m 35cm	3500m =	3km 500m
100mm =	10cm	280cm =	2m 80cm	2900m =	2km 900m
230mm =	23cm	307cm =	3m 7cm	4270m =	4km 270m
320mm =	32cm	199cm =	1m 99cm	1050m =	1km 50m

B

4kg 500g =	4500g	2l 400ml =	2400ml	8cm =	80mm
3kg 250g =	3250g	3l 250ml =	3250ml	7m 50cm =	750cm
1kg 100g =	1100g	4l 50ml =	4050ml	3750g =	3kg 750g
2kg 50g =	2050g	1l 90ml =	1090ml	1460ml =	1l 460ml

C

$\frac{1}{2}$ kilogram =	500g	$\frac{1}{2}$ litre =	500ml	$\frac{1}{2}$ kilometre =	500m
$\frac{1}{4}$ kilogram =	250g	$\frac{1}{4}$ litre =	250ml	$\frac{1}{4}$ kilometre =	250m
$\frac{3}{4}$ kilogram =	750g	$\frac{3}{4}$ litre =	750ml	$\frac{3}{4}$ kilometre =	750m
$\frac{1}{10}$ kilogram =	100g	$\frac{1}{10}$ litre =	100ml	$\frac{1}{10}$ kilometre =	100m
$\frac{1}{5}$ kilogram =	200g	$\frac{1}{5}$ litre =	200ml	$\frac{1}{5}$ kilometre =	200m

D

Write to the nearest cm.

29mm	3cm	32mm	3cm	77mm	8cm	85mm	9cm

Write to the nearest m.

485cm	5m	300cm	3m	509cm	5m	550cm	6m

Write to the nearest kg.

1kg 200g	1kg	2kg 690g	3kg	3kg 250g	3kg	4kg 500g	5kg

E Find the cost of

6m at 15p per metre	90p	5kg at 14p per kg	70p	3l at 30p per l	90p
$3\frac{1}{2}$m at 20p per metre	70p	$2\frac{1}{2}$kg at 30p per kg	75p	500ml at 50p per l	25p
50cm at 90p per metre	45p	$\frac{1}{4}$kg at £1.20 per kg	30p	100ml at £2 per l	20p
25cm at 40p per metre	10p	100g at £1.00 per kg	10p	$1\frac{1}{2}$l at 30p per $\frac{1}{2}$l	90p
$1\frac{1}{4}$m at 60p per metre	75p	200g at 40p per kg	8p	250ml at 70p per $\frac{1}{2}$l	35p

F Write in digits the time shown on each clock using a.m. or p.m.

morning times

afternoon times

8.16 a.m.	10.38 a.m.	12.22 p.m.	4.49 p.m.

G

How many days in		1 hour =	60min	How long is it from	
December	31	$\frac{1}{2}$h =	30min	8.45 a.m. to 9.10 a.m.	25min
September	30	$\frac{1}{4}$h =	15min	3.54 p.m. to 4.20 p.m.	26min
August	31	$\frac{3}{4}$h =	45min	10.56 a.m. to 12.15 p.m.	1h 19min
November	30	1 day =	24 hours	11.38 a.m. to midday	22min
March?	31	1 week =	7 days	9.00 a.m. to 3.00 p.m.?	6h

Full list of Schofield & Sims Mental Arithmetic books

Pupil books

Mental Arithmetic Introductory Book	ISBN 978 07217 0798 3
Mental Arithmetic 1	ISBN 978 07217 0799 0
Mental Arithmetic 2	ISBN 978 07217 0800 3
Mental Arithmetic 3	ISBN 978 07217 0801 0
Mental Arithmetic 4	ISBN 978 07217 0802 7
Mental Arithmetic 5	ISBN 978 07217 0803 4
Mental Arithmetic 6	ISBN 978 07217 0804 1

Answer books

Mental Arithmetic Introductory Book Answers	ISBN 978 07217 0853 9
Mental Arithmetic 1 Answers	ISBN 978 07217 0805 8
Mental Arithmetic 2 Answers	ISBN 978 07217 0806 5
Mental Arithmetic 3 Answers	ISBN 978 07217 0807 2
Mental Arithmetic 4 Answers	ISBN 978 07217 0808 9
Mental Arithmetic 5 Answers	ISBN 978 07217 0809 6
Mental Arithmetic 6 Answers	ISBN 978 07217 0810 2

Teacher's Guide

Mental Arithmetic Teacher's Guide	ISBN 978 07217 1389 2

Free downloads

A range of free downloads is available from the Schofield & Sims website (www.schofieldandsims.co.uk). These downloads may be used to support pupils in their learning, both in school and at home. They include the following items:

- two **Mental Arithmetic** Entry Tests to help you choose the best book for each individual

- an Achievement Award certificate for each **Mental Arithmetic** book

- Maths Facts downloads to provide a quick reference tool

- a National Curriculum Chart to show how each book supports the programmes of study.